WHEELS

ALSO BY KWAME DAWES

POETRY

Resisting the Anomie
Progeny of Air
Prophets
Jacko Jacobus
Requiem
Shook Foil
Mapmaker
Midland
New and Selected Poems
Bruised Totems
I Saw Your Face
Wisteria Twilight Songs from the Swamp Country
Brimming
Impossible Flying
Gomer's Song
Hope's Hospice
Back of Mount Peace

ANTHOLOGIES

Wheel and Come Again: An Anthology of Reggae Poetry
Red

FICTION

A Place to Hide
She's Gone
Bivouac

DRAMA

One Love

NONFICTION

Natural Mysticism: Towards a New Reggae Aesthetic
Talk Yuh Talk: Interviews with Anglophone Caribbean Poets
Bob Marley: Lyrical Genius
Twenty: South Carolina Poetry Fellows
A Far Cry from Plymouth Rock: A Personal Narrative

WHEELS

POEMS

KWAME DAWES

P E E P A L   T R E E

First published in Great Britain in 2011
Peepal Tree Press Ltd
17 King's Avenue
Leeds LS6 1QS
UK

ISBN 13:9781845231422

Supported by
ARTS COUNCIL
ENGLAND

CONTENTS

2
Measure

3
Brimming

5

Home, Again

1

WHEELS

Your young men shall see visions and
your old men shall see dreams

Acts 2: 17 (and Joel 2: 28)

OUR COLOSSAL FATHER, AGAIN

Sob, heavy world,
Sob as you spin.

W.H. Auden

1

The portrait painter's art works like faith that turns
the wafer, the decanter of wine into something else.

A dragon swaggers through the portal
of our century, striding into a gothic sky.

2

In another country, olive groves
and gleaming mosques are pulverized to dust.

Outside the white courtyards, bloody streets
fade after sudden explosions.

3

He is a throwback to grand lawgivers
who stretched their arms over the world.

We will remember him for his Augustinian self-denial,
the last beer he drank, and his mealy-mouthed sermons.

4

His prophets pour oil that rises
in flood across the marbled floor.

Better a good name than costly oil,
the day of death than the day of birth.

In the faint light of dusk he seems
to be walking on water.

LAST DAYS

Rain and ashes seal my lips
                                        Allen Ginsberg

In the season of drought and hurricane,
this stiff earth cracks and the spawned
eggs of mosquitoes burst into a plague
of coughs and side stitches. Every wild bird
predicts a plague of woes. All around us
the whisper is of "Last Days", the coming
of the end, and the tyranny of present danger.

December 21, 2005, Marvin Williams,
ex-Drill Sergeant and born-again Arkansas
cotton-picker, remembers the morning he
was bumped from the airliner that flamed
over Lockerbie. *Blessed*, he says, trying
to calculate the debts he still owes.
Why was he kept; for what?

The dragonflies are dying,
and in the suburbs the pandemic
runs amok. Our bodies betray us
and the summer's heat warms
the sea, as deep as plummet sounds.
In the desert it rains in deluge,
while the glaciers vanish from mountains.
The stars die a million years ago.

On a beach in Bahia,
a congregation in white descends
to the water's edge, singing. The surf lips
the disembowelled carcasses of small
animals. A rash of flowers eddies
on the swollen surface like a garland of prayer.

Better go to the house of mourning
than to the house of feasting.

WHEELS

Ezekiel saw a wheel a-turning,
Way in the middle of the air,
A wheel within a wheel a-turning...

The gangly televangelist suffered
the insults of schoolmates,
but promises no rancour in the afterlife.

He still looks the geek – clumsy, heavy-headed,
bloated chin and a way of talking
with an auctioneer's impatience and alarm.

He longs to dream the vision of beasts
with double wings, one set outstretched,
the other folded over their groins;

the spirit of the beasts caught in the centrifuge
of wheels interlocking, wheels turning and turning,
the spark of roaming eyes caught in the rims.

This is how God used to fill the sky:
touch red embers to the lips of prophets
and teach the naysayer penitence.

The televangelist is waiting, his body stiff
beside his snoring wife, the pale cilia on his skin,
alert antennae to catch every errant wind of faith.

EAT

He said, "Son of man, eat what is given to you; eat this scroll..."
Ezekiel 3:1

If you feed me with thin parchment
made from the papyrus of ancient rivers
that green the desert's edge,

and if you feed me the torn sheets, stained
in sepia from mashed berries of old lands,

and if you feed me the bitter taste
of your commanding, my belly
burning with the acid of your ire,

and if you force me to feed on
the burdens of your heart,

and if I bend over the toilet bowl,
the juices in my stomach churning
on a fevered southern night,

I will be the dry brush
set aflame by your truth.

A man must know when night's
reflux – the throat burning
with half-digested meals – is the heat
of the spirit blessing his head.

Lord, don't let me eat your words, no more.
Lord, just can't eat them words, no more.

SEA GULLS OVER TWO NOTCH ROAD

You teach me the terror of death.
My belly stretches. *Be full*, you say,
with the indiscretion of your burden.
Save yourself by walking to the exiles
camped on the Kebar river, and disgorge
yourself of the curse of silence. Lay on them
the weight of knowledge and truth.

Sea gulls darken the sky, shadows
settling over the parking lot. The sound
of wings and turning wheels fills
the electric air. I have been walking
with the unsteady limp of a cripple,
my crushed right ankle fused
in an angle of pain. The air
carries my bones over asphalt.

It is hard to hear the sin of a nation's
turning. To quiet this I try to chatter
and tell of the gulls alighting in my yard.
A dry wind fills my mouth, sticking tongue to palate.

RITUALS BEFORE THE POEM

In terror they will drink water grudgingly
                                                    Ezekiel 4

Before the poem comes like a word from a brazen sky
the poet must lie on his side for a year
eating only dry bread and measured bowls of water.

The poet must pour sand over grass and build
the walls of his city. The poet must surround
the walls with the offence of guns; and for days
upon days starve the city of all its music.

The poet's tongue will grow heavy and his
limbs will be bound with cords so he cannot
move. He will quarrel with God about
the meaning of poetry. The poet will beg for mercy,
lying on his other side for a hundred and ninety days,
his body scarred with the wounds he inflicts on his family.

All this a poet does before a poem so that
when he walks out in midwinter, his face
will be smooth, his eyes will have the quiet resignation
we call peace, and his satchel will be full
of whimsical lyrics about the colour green
and the sounds a whore makes in her dreams.

BALDNESS

Is this merely practice?
Some believe in heaven,
some in rest.

Ellen Bryant Voigt

That morning I took a machete
and sharpened the edge white
against a seasoned rockstone.

Then I shaved my face, clumps
falling gently on my feet.

Burnt, the smell is sweet like flesh
cooked. A sticky mess remains.

Tossed into the sky, it falls again
then trundles in balls across the land.

But chopped into sharp darts
by the machete it makes lakes black.

You learn to keep a fist full
in your breast pocket for luck.

A bald man must have evidence
of his shame always with him.

That morning I woke expecting
to see emaciated bodies
withered and wildly attired;
fathers eating their children,
children feasting on their fathers;

but all I found were caskets too heavy
for pallbearers and a nation
swollen with its pleasure.

I had no words for such a people
so I went back to sleep.

My head was naked and cold
and the engine of angels' wings
hummed in my chest.

GENOCIDE, AGAIN

If a man were to wake in Sun City,
he would smell the truth of prophecy.
Those close by will die by machete blow,
those far away will die of the plague,
and those who are spared
will know the famine of orphaned days –
the youth wandering motherless
through the hollow houses tucked
into the overgrown valleys and hills,
the yam vines choked by the verdant
bush, and the earth swallowing
the wet stain of a dead body.

The famine will soon destroy
the remnant, leaving an impossible
cavity in the nation. A man wakes
to the truth that sometimes God's
word smells like the rotting flesh
of murdered bodies scattered
among broken incense bowls, cold
wet fireplaces, strewn clothes,
splatters of blood on the floor,
an overturned pot, rice grains hardening
in the stale air and an empty leather sandal.

IDOLATRY

If you stand in an open field long enough –
the sky inflamed like the bursting flesh
of a corrupting corpse – you will be dragged
by the hair, your neck straining
against your skull, and lifted to places
that would turn the sweet weight
of a masticated scroll in your belly
into an acidic curdling, rising like a flood.

Scratch the wall with spit-wet fingers
until you see the hieroglyphs
of desire etched into the gloomy
walls. In the middle, the host
seethes neglected. We pamper our pets
with holy awe. They give all back.

Weep, you women, so Tammuz
will come and fill you with babies,
soften the brittle skin and give you
a new achievement after so many
years. Weep, you women, for Tammuz.

At our back is the image of our
uncertainty but before us the sun
returns as always. How reliable
are its rituals, how salient
its prophecies. A man cannot be blamed
for falling down to feel the warmth
left in the earth after the passing
of the old sun. A man cannot.

MARKED

The poet stands beside the soldiers,
he is dressed in cloths of yellow;

in one hand a bucket of sepia ink sloshes
like the blood of protection; in the other,
the brush, its bristles gathered to a point.

Outside, the world will wonder at the wrath
of sweet, peacemaking God, who has
his history of filling the streets
with the mutilated body of sinners,
who understands the language
of stinking corpses, who knows
mercy and the absence of memory,
whose sorrow was heaviest
over one slender body stretched
and split on a slab of wood.

The poet must step into the city,
bewildered by the wickedness
of the people, to write haiku
on the foreheads of those who lament,
lines of revelation in the senna
hieroglyphs – a mark, a brand,
a stroke of hope on the lintels
of their faces. The poet must weep
when he returns, his linen
garments brown with the blood
of promise, his feet sticky
with the spilled blood of despair.

A soh it go.

THE GLORY HAS LEFT THE TEMPLE

for Gabriel Garcia Marquez

To tell it, I must call it a dream.

A dream on the Caribbean coast of Columbia
where a beautiful black man serves
thick omelettes, messy with onions and mushrooms
to an assortment of mavericks – dock workers,
professors, maids, three police officers,
five whores and a clutch of lawyers at midnight,
sopping up the curdling rum in their bellies
with thick chunks of white doughy bread.

Antonio, the black chef in flowing linen,
has a hand jutting from his belly
to hold hot coals, and above his head
the interlocking, whirling wheels
with a thousand eyes blinking back tears
but following our every movement.

The earth has grown weary with too much blood.

Everyone is checking the casualties
like the scores of football matches.

I could call it a dream, a kind of
Marquezian apocalypse, the memoir
of a novelist being handed the reams
of paper on which he will prophecy
to the wind. Instead, I will admit
the truth: I have been sitting in a hot
room smelling rich with incense
and the sweat of priests who have lost

the language to comfort the bereaved –
priests whose idols have crumbled
to dust. I am listening to the wind,
to the voice in the wind telling me
to write it all down. So I do.

HARBOUR

So I stepped indoors watching the dust
climb the shaft of light lazily,
waiting until dusk. I dug my way
through the wall, covered my head
and felt my way through the city,
towards the docks where the first schooners
from Curaçao were dipping
their anchors secretly and the hushed
hymns of the captives rolled over
the water, their scent a long
dense epoch of despair. The watchman,
his face weather-worn, spoke
a Gullah tongue in the light drizzling
noise of ashes on water. The days
go by and his every vision turns
to nothing. From here the green
smell of the market makes a forest
of this city and the pink hint
of dawn could not be the flame
of God reckoning. The watchman
points me to the schooner, tells me
to go, tells me that from now on
all things shall be fulfilled, and
on the bulwark of Fort Sumter
the small dispatch of troops
stumbles into the thick granite walls.

Charleston, SC, 2006

WISE MAN

Looking for a god to come from outer space,
So much careless Ethiopians have gone astray

Toots and the Maytals

I long to be the wise man
in the shadows.

Problem is in discernment.

The women wear jewels
and wave veils to trap
us careless Ethiopians,
while the prophets amass
in full make-up
on the television sound stage
to predict with miraculous knowledge
to the viewing millions.

Chances are you will find
among the devout congregation
staring dumbly at the flat screens
at least one with a cancerous toe,
or a foul-mouthed spouse,
or a predilection for porn,
or a sharp backache
waiting for the screen
to speak its name,
to speak her pain.

The wise man in the shadows
whispers the end of things
while the world continues

the pattern of beasts
feeding on worms
to be feasts for the worms.

Amen.

AMONG THE DITHERING FEATHERS

There is providence in a sparrow's fall,
but around me here in the vacant
parking lot of Khols, it is snowing
the feathers of gulls, a plague of them
rising raucously into the dull sky –
the smell of beached fish
in the air though we are ninety miles
from the sea. I have been losing hold
of dreams of late; something tells
me that they are rank with prophecy.

This morning the freight train rattling
along Two Notch Road shook me up.
My throat flamed with words half-
spoken. I waited for the settling
of the dream into a language
I could recollect. Nothing. Now
among the dithering feathers,
the chill of a slow dawn, I sense
the weight of sight; a truth
caught in the fantastic chaos
of this moment. Still, nothing;
just a sliver of some old dead
poet's musing, something about
divinities, ends, providence
and the bodies strewn in a hall
fetid as a mist-filled battlefield.

MANIFEST DESTINY

I may be a false prophet, but god bless me, at least
I have something to say…
                                    Nance Van Winckel

At day's end a nation cannot be blamed
for its righteous wrath, fat as it is.
Fat, after all, is God's gift, not so?
This obese land must have made
some deal with God; nothing burns
here, no desolation like a land
broken by cataclysm.
A people cannot be blamed for
their clear-eyed instinct for the right,
for the studied assurance
of their pontifications. After all,
the blessings arrive bountifully
and the priests have come upon
the mystery of His grace: their
seamless linen, their panelled homes —
all the proof of their selection.
A wretched fat woman walks the streets
announcing the end of all things,
the wasted burning of the fat vine;
but she is, quite simply, demented,
and will be gathered up soon,
and given a bowl of soup and warm shelter.

HISTORY, TOO

The teller sits on a cold beach,
the black murmur of so many languages
breaking against the muddy coastline.
Beyond this barrier island is history
and the unspoken lament.

The ground is stuffed with the bones
of those who never made it to Charleston,
then further inland, scattered across the continent,
buried with shells, beads, slivers
of wood; the earth's belly has settled:
no upheavals, just the calm
acceptance of drying bodies.

I cannot travel towards the coast
without hearing the long song
of the dead Africans. The island grows
narrow; the coast slowly eaten away.
Winter is a calm season here,
And the earth is warm – a shelter.

The teller speaks a parable of stones.
The ocean is nonchalant.

Sullivan's Island, SC

THE SECRET CARPENTRY

Further away, forgiveness is easier; a face
penitent with regret, stoic and resolved,
mouthing the jargon of clean, precise,
well-reasoned bloodshed – a voice tutored
in the art of eliminating options, making
the logic of power seductive. Those are
the forgivable sins. After all, how are we
to doubt when we have not smelt the hint
of stale liquor on their breaths, caught
them in some cute hypocrisy, found
them out for lies they have told
or the cruel cut of their laughter
at some hapless fool? Power feeds
our hopelessness. To make monsters
of our foes, we rely on dogma, avoid nuance.
Still, a poet sits on an ancient
marble block staring at the pale
blue sky, scratching poems, soft
ghazals in a notepad. He is counting
echoes while calculating the cost
of next month's rent in US dollars.
He has learned the meter of elegies –
so many buried, their faces sallow.
He still feels the terror
of concussions when he walks. For him
monsters carry the currency of dogma.
He has no taste for dogma, now.
He searches out, instead, the secret carpentry
of poems hoping that they will last
beyond the presidents, the envoys,
the ambassadors, the ayatollahs,
the advisors, the martyrs, the rabbis,

the shamans, the bloodied freedom
fighters. The poet knows his own
monstrosity: the vanity of songs
in a world full of the dying. Night
crawls across the earth's surface, a shadow
devouring the last morsels of light.

THE END HAS COME

The dead should just shut up. Already
they've ruined the new-plowed field:
it looks like a grave.
Ellen Bryant Voigt

In the mountains the shamefaced
shaven people will moan
like doves of the valley.

I am the clumsy orator whose words
fall out like wet leaves and form
a mulch on the ground.

There is a break in the journey
for revelation to be voiced.

The seer wakes in the morning
believing in calamity, translating
an ice storm as the hand of God.

I am stumbling around, following
the seer who walks through the city
announcing the end of things.

I must not welcome such ruin. How sweet
is the ritual sunrise of this living earth,
and death is not peace but the loss
of the sweet pleasures of the flesh.

Someday, soon, I will sit among the remnant
high in the Appalachian Mountains
and moan like a dove of the valley,

asking for a quiet death in fading light,
and all these words will be the compost
rotting in the sunless corners of my garden.

CUCKOLD

The tender man makes cuckoldry holiness,
the pure penance of the wounded.

He rehearses the salvaging of a discarded
woman, cleaning the thick layer

of birth-dross from her skin, her umbilicus
long and tattered at the end — the sign

of abandonment. He bathes her,
dresses her in soft cloths, feeds her,

teaches her the language of devotion
and gratitude. So her whorish

ingratitude (which is inevitable, we know)
is the flagellation that sets off

in his under-skin, the glow of a saint.
Eventually she will return to his bosom,

fall on his breast, tell him of the wayward
paths she has taken: the journeys

she has made along the paved rainbow
alleys of the city; the men she has fucked;

the men she has dressed in crushed linen;
the men she has walked barefoot with

on the beach, making careless love
beside the rotting carcasses of beached

dolphins. And they will weep together,
her hurt, her regret, his grace, his love

softening her vulva to a welcome wetness,
and their lovemaking will enact the ancient

rituals of return.

THE GAP

There is arrogance in the dusty-haired prophet
strutting across the screen, bible flapping
like a dead bird in his palms. Clean lines,
the way the suit falls on his shoulders,
the even symmetry of his shaved head –
this fine man causes the camera to linger
on the amen corner, beatific faces neatly
entranced. The prophet times his pronouncement
with his arrival at the back drop
of the good flag, the power of a nation,
and he asks, *Who will stand in the gap?*
– as if the wrath of a parent has time
for one clumsy child while the others
disappear from the tale; as if every
word written in the floppy bird of a testament
was meant for this nation; as if
the narrative of history ends here;
and we are so proud of our many sins –
our abominations a sign of our election –
that when we weep it is with the warm
delusions of promise, the assurance
that all things have conspired to meet us
here in this instance – as if the ordination
of our daily rituals of eating, shitting,
sleeping are enshrined in the mind of God.
The prophet is well-paid for the one single
miracle of his presence – the art of relevance
in the face of inertia, the bleak despair
of the commonness of our humanity, the absurd
pageant of our days of failure, our teeth on edge,
our bellies distended by the sour grapes we've eaten.

THE POET
For FD

I know yours is a stoic sense of irony –
at least that is the face to your resignation
to the law of the Philistines: *Who gives a fuck
about quality, these days?* In this fresh
millennium, the fowls have come home
to roost and there is no justice –
mediocrity rules, genius poets
supplanted by the reparation-spouting,
lazy-rhyme-making (*how many words
rhyme with reality?*) table-turners.
All these modern blacks, the axe-mouthed
women, who can blame them for taking
the gifts proffered? Who would expect
them to do the noble thing and say
give it to the Anglo-white poet
with chronic backaches and a genetic
disposition to Beethoven and Bach
and other things classical? His verse
you see, is staid, wonderfully crafted
and holds dear all that we've admired
all these years. He rails in sturdy iambics
against the harlots preening themselves –
their skins, their breasts – for the Assyrians.
Better, he says, to speak of the indulgence
of blood, of the gracelessness of women
who seduce in the red season. Better to play
the prophet being written into the canon,
that testament that will outlast fads, generations,
the false fleeting foolishness of Mammon.
Better to build the myths of standards and pray
to be discovered some resurrection day
among the ruins of libraries many years hence.

EZEKIEL CHAPTER TWENTY-FIVE

The adulterer prayed: *Take away the hunger*
from my eyes. And in three days the fruit
stall in the soft entrails of the city
became a cluster of dry wood and bone,
the bulbous plums, erect bananas,
fat sweating paw-paw rotted;
and the parade of open skirts, big
thighs and mindless breasts became
the stern reproach of a grandmother's
starched cotton, the architecture of girdles
and sensible stockings multiplying
themselves on the city's streets.
The lake was like glass, the mountains
covered in blood; and all choice meat
dropped into the open pot, simmered
in its own juices, the scum,
a rippling of fat gathering
on the surface. No wonder the priest
let it all burn to the brittle wood
and bone fuel of the fire, leaving
that sticky black residue of flesh
caramelized – *Oh how sweet the fat is!*
No wonder the pot melted until nothing
remained but the blackened bones
and the testament of how the earth
will face its sun. The adulterer
is learning the sterile futility of purity,
how the absence of sacrifice is no answer
to desire; how blood must be shed,
entrails exposed to the sun
so that the sweet stench of sacrifice
can rise slowly up into the pink vulva of the sky.

THE CURSE

Curse a man as if he is a country;
curse him with drought and blight,
with long terraces of graves where bodies
lie piled up, eyes wide open
under the smoky sky; curse him
with disease and bad fortune,
with massive debts, disloyal neighbours,
with crabby whores and sullen priests;
curse him with forty years of exile
at the mercy of some alien land;
curse him as if his sin is as voracious
as a nation's – a bellyful of indiscretions –
and the wounds of civilization
blistering into boils in the skin.
Curse him this way, and know that
only the fear of an afterlife,
the tutor of insecurity about hell
or heaven, will make him pause
long enough to know you are not planting
a garland of praise on his head.
For all great men – dons, gorgons,
maximum leaders, war lords,
ayatollahs, presidents and kings –
know that only the lofty
will cause God Almighty to deign
to speak a curse on one man
as if he is a nation. Only a fallen
angel would warrant such tribute.
We die, we rot; all that is left
is the path we scorched into the land.

SHEEP

All ye like sheep…

People who repress desires often become, suddenly,
hypocrites. The shepherds have abandoned
their sheep; they now smell of rose water
and the musk of good beer; they are a fat
generation, and they sit above the scattered
flock somewhere on the rock flowering with
elegant panelled houses. Sometimes a nation
forgets the rituals of mercy – after all,
the flanks of the meaty sheep now press against
the skinny ones who are pushed from
the succulent grass. They starve. It is
the order of nature. Desire hangs like
a shroud over our days. At the creek's
edge, a mile from the sea, where the water
is close to its spring, some wade
through mud to the cleaner depths
to drink, then they wallow in the shallows,
stirring the silt, until the weak swallow
a mouthful of dirt. Those who repress
desire grow brutal in the half-light.
They devour the flesh of the poor;
they carry values like a mantra,
and declare their holiness in the copious
girth of their thighs. Does anyone need
to say that judgment will fall on them?
After all, poets have forgotten the dialect
of foresight – we, too, are hungry,
and the cold institutionalized holiness
of this nation has silenced us. Repress desire,
and carry the horror of deceit in our tongues.
This, too, will not last. This too must pass.

DRY BONES

Here is a grave pun, how the cure of the tomb
is a sacrament for the afterlife of wings
and tanned leather of flesh stretched over bone.
At its core is the agnostic straddling of doubt.
But dust to dust has done just fine
all these centuries; the thing is to find
the mineral grace of dust, its healing –
another pun. There is no pun in prophesy –
the imperative to a waking woman, sending
her into the broken graveyard where
the earth has dried after the upheaval
of bones by storm and the shifting
of soil; no play in commanding a man
to stand over the dry rot of broken bones –
the scattering of a tribe – to say to this
desolate land something that will
turn a dry cough, a scratchy throated
voice into magic – the cadence
of blood and tendon, the fleshing
of the rotted – to say, "Bones, come
together!" What happens to the pieces
of shrapnel, the rusted blades,
the residue of steel lodged in bones
when bones gather themselves
to walk? Anyone who hears
this command, who feels the wetness
of hope in the voice calling her,
has seen the destruction of her people –
the fallowing of her land, emptied
of the living; she knows the sound
of steel on flesh and bone, the pleas of the fallen.

PATIENCE

For Sudan

If you wait long enough after the command
and if the rain stays in the mountains

while the sun sucks every shoot from the earth
and the starving crows have scoured

every broken village, every burnt-out farmstead;
the searcher of bones can find femurs,

skulls and curved vertebrae by the glint
of sunlight on the blanched surface.

There is no need to sniff out
the sweet sourness of human death –

wait long enough and all tasks become
ordinary, simple rituals of the civil

servant. This is how a nation is cleansed
of its memory, memory of the overcast

dawn filled with the snowfall of ash;
and the shimmering cry of the singer

on the Western Hill, his voice cutting
through the thick gloom, calling all the birds

to a fast of flesh and the intoxication
of blood – that feast that left the courtyards

bare and brilliant by the time of the celebrations,
as if all had found themselves ensnared

in the dreams of food and fat cooks
chopping quarter moons of garlic and rolling

mountains of leavened dough, dreams
of fruit bursting with the perfume

of readiness. But the houses
are hollow, the towers have no sentries,

the stones are dark with the sun-drunk
packs of bewildered dogs. This is how

a nation forgets its loss, and hopes foolishly
for peace to come each new morning.

If you wait long enough, all murders
will have lost their scream, all bloodlines

forgotten, all tribes scattered, all scores
settled, all bones cleaned of the memory of pain.

2

THE MEASURE

THE MEASURE

If dreams carry the illogic of our fears,
then a man standing on the edge of a forest
with a measuring rod cradled in the curve
of his shoulder – the smooth cylinder
pressing against the back of his head –
would be some kind of news, cutting through
all our meandering daydreams: the mirage
of laughing women; the soft throat
of tears from a Dylan song cast
into a molasses pool of Rock Steady
from a backroom smelling of talc and carbolic
and the saltiness of a woman's sweat –
her rituals of taking, lovemaking,
aching and quietly breaking in this reggae.

All of this would be pushed back far
enough to let us see in the man's skin
the inscriptions on temple surfaces:
the jambs, the porticoes, the alcoves,
the parapets and the finished
stone of the altars where flesh
is broken, left to heal before the fire –
all that blood and the holy rituals.

In dreams a man can find a language
for loss, a cantor for the laments
of his days. This is how a dream
carries tenderly through the night.

PRAYER

The holy emperor, caught in the quagmire of war,
gangrened sores, the rotting heads
of the slaughtered, sniffs the scent of decay
on the plains stretched out beneath
the lyric mountains. A king can fear
death, calculate loss and imagine
the martyrdom of bravery, but the dizzy
promises of heroism, the rituals
of retribution, the pragmatism
of wartime do not hold the small
man; he vanishes – it is his way
to vanish, either to find himself
among the lions, or to pray.
The enemy waits; the news is simple:
the lineage of kings is enough to turn
Ethiopia into the dry track of miracles
when men quarrel with God and stones
talk back. A servant said that when,
in nineteen seventeen-four, they came
for him, he first pleaded with fate,
wondered at the betrayal of his people,
calculated the legacy of his works,
and wailed that he did not deserve
this. Then he fell to his knees
and prayed – intoning psalms.
He'd prayed a warrior's prayer forty years
before – the power of the trinity
making deals with a dealing God
in the dark temple cut into the rocks.
Come morning, the empire was splintered,
and he was ready for the empire in his heart,
the empire he carried with him to Bath,

to exile while Europe balked. The empire
moved in that slow march across lands,
over oceans into the dark shelter of exile.
But it would grow again, baptized in prayer,
the simple prayer of piety of a king,
only to break again in the unsteady hands
of this warrior king whose prayers
now wither on his lips, then fall
like leaves at his feet.

YISHAK

I, Yishak the scribe, have learned the dialect of wind.
Where there is sand and stone, a lyric is written
to be collected in scriptures inked into the skin
of lambs. The scribes work in the stone silence
of transportation. The Word arrives with simple
truths. It is as if time has hesitated here in this land,
and the priests in their robes, the tangle of cloth
wrapped around their necks, smell of old blood
and the business of dealing with God. In the Trinity
Cathedral in Addis, the priest quarrels
in quick Amharic with the guide – he wants more
money from the journalists gawking at the dark pink
granite tomb of the Emperor. Sometimes
a hermit wearing matted locks and the skin
of goats will ascend to the plateau of the city
to speak prophecies to the congregants.
The emperor, he says, comes not from dirt
but from blood and the sacred narratives
of scribes like Yishak – the orderer of things.

At the temple door, blood congeals.
A new elaborate crown of inlaid gold
and yards of animal pelts, lions' manes
and the feathers of ostriches are laid heavily
on the miniature monarch; the *k'ibrat*
of the Holy Ghost flows through the oiled
hands of the Patriarch, roams through the silk
sky and anoints the livid head of the king.

The scribe is a poet and maker of myths.
If the scribe came through the eucalyptus groves
and announced through phlegm and broken teeth

that when Sheba, the queen, travelled through
desert to Jerusalem to find Solomon, she found
wisdom and the providence of a womb filled
with the earnest of his seed, we must understand
that this epic of journeys on camels through dust
is the making of empire. Every king must know
the narratives of his making. I, Yishak, serve kings.

Yes, I, Yishak, will listen to the voice of the hills
and trace a path from stone to stone, the relics
of legitimacy, the myths of purpose. Tomorrow,
the artisans and poets will turn the scripture into soul
and a nation will have a claim to the finger of God.
This is how the earth turns holy, how dark men grow
lengthy beards dripping with the oil of anointing,
how we find grounding in the shifting land.

This, then, is how an emperor will stride the blast of a warring
world, gather the mystique of unction about him;
how the death of our monarch leaves the rotted stump
of an amputated branch twitching with the dumb madness
of ghosts. A fable swirls in the echoing hills:
it is now the cloak that warms the nation.

LASTA MOUNTAINS

There among the rocks of Roha
the stone obeys the chisel and muscle
of the mason. The land is bare
of all shapers of stone as they have been
summoned to the rugged hills,
there to cut out courtyards,
hollow halls and shelters
for the ark of the covenant
with its twelve pillars.
Men carve into the stone
the dialect of the tribes:
eleven sepulchres, eleven
singing places where the priests
may lead the Ge'ze chants,
hurling their bodies in dance
there on the Lasta mountains.

Born at the foothills
of such miracles, who can blame
a people for their simple dignity –
the quiet presence of lions?

The fine-limbed runners
do not stare to the ground,
but hold their heads like antennae
facing the hills from whence
comes all help. It was there
in 1936 that the Emperor
took shelter after a chaotic
retreat and, rather than weep,
he prayed for eight days
before the long march

through exile and into
return. There in the echo
of the cool sanctuary
where prayers swirled
as old as David's despair,
the empire hung in the balance.
This kingdom of bones
and broken stones
taught him in the language
of permanence cloaked
in the uncertain
fluidity of destiny.

MENELIK II

So those latter-day Romans
dismissed the canopies of purple,
the golden footstools, the crowns,
the elaborate titles, the complex faith,
the annals collected in tomes beneath
the shelter of ancient rock;
they called them savages
pretending to humanity –
genus thoughtless mimics,
as if they were years
past the blood sacrifice,
divination and monstrous
brutality. Enterprising Italians
indulged the monkey kings
and his court of chattering nobles,
plying them with false promises,
succulent lamb, cheap wine
and rusted weapons. It would not
be long, they calculated,
before guile would tame them
and then, as all good
colonisers must, they would
drag them from their delusions
of grandeur, their stubborn pride,
their brutish rituals.

In 1896 the nations hovered over Ethiopia;
Menelik counted on the myths
of his fine tribalism to beat them back,
so that the name Adowa would haunt
those Romans for decades after.
With the righteousness of martyrdom,

Menelik taught us the foolishness of Europe,
while the Ark of the Covenant
glowed in the hill-cave monasteries
guarded by priests. A new scripture
unfolded. Soon the poor, starving, would learn
to feed on the scrolls of the scribes;
an empire stretched inexorably
towards its own implosion – the snake
would eat its tail, the Emperor
holding his sceptre saw it rust –
the slow canker of worms,
the decay, the constant decay.

In Menelik Square, a too great man
dwarfs the elevated horse,
hooves beating the air, the pure
triumph of the hero.

THE MAGIC OF MONARCHY

Come next year, the rains
shroud the palace with silence.
It is as if the Emperor has travelled,
but worse. Now cows graze
on the palace lawns, there's no fanfare
and all ceremony is down to
the ritual of an Emperor
dithering his painful way through
the echoing hallways, before
they gather him and place him
in the villa surrounded by
soldiers. There in the chapel
a servant reads the psalmists,
the prophets, the patriarchs –
all fallen men awaiting the jackals
slinking through the broken walls
of the ruined palace. He prays
with trembling lips while silence
hangs over the world. It is
the season of new things:
the courtiers are dead,
the nobles slaughtered,
the ministers, the sweet, sweet
children – all gone, while soldiers
wait for the magic of majesty
to make them die.
The world will not understand
the quiet of an empty court,
the emperor's thinning beard
and the blankness in his eyes,
like Jesus who knows that silence
turns the ordinary to the divine;

eyes that see the cross ahead.
Jesus, though, timed it well,
or at least the crowd was afire.
Here, the palace is dead,
the people have returned
to the routine of starvation,
the city has lost its way.

TEN IMPERIAL RULES
Notes of a disgruntled palace servant

1

Collect bad ministers, keep them close.
Give grandiose gifts to these – a good
minister must have much to lose.
Collect bad ministers so you may shine;
chaos demands the salve of order.

2

Teach absurd rituals,
encourage slavish practices,
bowing and scraping,
bobbing heads, elastic necks,
the backward retreat,
a shuffle. By contrast
acts of benevolence
will seem quite holy.

3

The only useful tyranny
is loyalty; avoid the stench
of reform, it splinters
a simple single sun
into galaxies,
a constellation of distracting
loyalties.

4

Let the poor know the hand
that feeds them by withholding
the hand that feeds them –
when the flies have darkened
their faces and the skeletons
stay bowed in the streets.

5

Teach love by the caress
of soft fingers, as if running
through the silk of a lion cub's
tawny fur, after the lingering
sting of a merciless slap.

6

Never speak loudly;
know the miserliness
of whispers, the magic
of silence; never speak
with the wise, only
listen so the wise
can imagine the depth
of your wisdom.
Treat words like the detritus
of thought, the debris
clogging streams in rainy

season; hoard words
in the brain: name
the ministry of words
The Office of Sanitation.

7

Always keep the ears clean,
digging out the wax
of rotten words. The ear
is the precious funnel,
the gilded grail
best left unclogged
by the debris of talkers.
The ear can discern
anarchies a province
away if kept
polished, clean, purged.

8

At the palace gates,
give extravagantly
to the poor, let them
fight over copper coins,
scraps of cloth and the oil
of the emperor's blessing.
Offer large gifts and promises
to the nobles at the filthy
back doors of the palace
in the gloom before night.

9

Arrive always with bombast
and alarums; remember
the throne adds dignity
only by contrast to abject
humility. A throne glows
in a sea of burlap.

10

Treat those who demur
to your gifts for the sake
of the people as corrupt.
Only friends will take
a bribe from a king.

FAITHFUL

Jah live, children, yeah
                                    Bob Marley

1

We, too, will not accept the fictions
arriving from abroad. The emperor,
our precious little man, the incarnate,
the hand of wrath, miracles
and hope, the surrogate father
for the fatherless and the fathers,
the armour over us, righteous Quixotic
slayer of giants, the stone the builders
refused, the conquering lion,
the tiny island that is *tallawah*,
the pebble rushing into Goliath's head,
the grace of Africa, the bearded man
with eyes of eternity, he with many names,
is dead? All messiahs
will walk through their Gethsemane,
face the treachery of Judas,
stir rumours of unlikely death,
but the mystery of conquest over death
is the right of all Messiahs.

2

Not even rumours of death
must pass the lips of the dread.
Now we know the lies
of Babylon will know no bounds;

now we know that the descendants
of King James and his diabolic
scribes will continue to debase
all truth; now we know
that the dead must bury
the dead, but Jah liveth
itinually: Jah must live!

3

> *If Jah didn't love I,*
> *Would I be around today*
> *Would I be around to say…*
>   Marley

Faith multiplies itself
and swells like yeast
in the heat of Kingston.
Our man, our little warrior,
why must they defame you,
why do they try
to confound the prophets?

4

> *…but I and I know*
> *dread it shall be dreader dread.*
>   Marley

Here in Kingston the disciples
gather in the upper studio
and wait for the *k'ibat*

of the holy Ghost which comes
in a simple liturgy of proverbs:

Fools say in their heart,
Rasta your God is dead…

Turn to the alchemy of dub;
make from the detritus
of the poor the golden hope
of reggae; the poor will
believe beyond the rumour.
Rasta liveth; our little man
cyaan dead, our little god.

IN TRANSIT
Rome, September 2005

Because they are Romans we will
call it the sickness of love, the taste
for desire's fluids, an addiction,
but what we mean is the tawdry
hold of a drug – colonialism –
attaches to the genes, and its
tenacious grip, a fusing to the cells,
rots generation after generation.
The fat, balding dictator, even
on the eve of his hanging
in the square, still dreams
himself to an erection,
while the boots of his lackeys
clatter helter-skelter
through the barren streets.
He dreams of the times of triumph
the Alexandrian pomp of phalanxes
of troops entering the centre
of Addis Ababa, the city of heathens
who must be tamed, ruled, ordered,
taught the nobility of God's
purest tongue. He dreams
as if he will wake to laurels
and the tributes of elephant
tusks, the hides of lions
and the bowing beards of the Abyssinians.
This ailment will not die
with the balding dictator;
his last speech, an arching
tribute to the myth of conquest,
leaves drops of gleaming spittle

on the lips of the future, their tongues
flick the drops into their blood
and it will carry that trace of greed,
the addiction of empire.

RASTA

The grand emperor of Harlem
with a Falmouth accent, thick
with raw molasses from the cane
factories, can smell out a legend.
Look to Africa is the prophecy,
and the Ethiope will birth
a hero, no, a messiah. And this Jamaican
Harlem man has read the Solomonic
line, knows the dignity of Abyssinia
and so learns the language of faith,
speaks it to the broken people
of Harlem. Africa is a land of princes,
Africa is the home of true pomp;
and all is couched in the cadence
of majesty and prophecy.
Despite Waugh with his girlie name
and Oxford colonial stain
going on about barefooted warriors
in their tarnished pomp and ceremony,
or something such, the world understands
the icon of miracles, and the beaten-
down Africans in Kingston's Dungle
can dream of a land, so far across the sea,
and an emperor to boot, a black man
with a mane of locks and eyes of steel
and golden sceptres – a tamer of lions.
The thick-necked Harlem emperor
learns that prophecy cannot
be taken back, and the world
will know the new skank
to a new rhythm and henceforth,
the chant *Jah*, will now be followed
by the response, *Rastafari,*
ever living, ever faithful, ever sure.

AFRICAN POSTMAN

For Solomon Ephraim Woolfe

> *Son, who is dat?*
> *Is de African Postman, Daddy*
> > Burning Spear

East from Addis Ababa, and then south
deep into the Rift Valley, I can hear the horns
trumpeting over the flat-roofed acacia trees,
see African women bend low with wood
heavy on their backs, and the cows, goats,
donkeys, mules, sheep, and horses snapped
into obedient herds by sprinting children,
move along the roadside. Life happens here.
I am travelling to the land I have heard about,
Sheshemane, the green place, five hundred acres
of Jah's benevolence, and I know now that
I long to hear the rootsman tell me how,
despite rumours of his passing, the natty
keeps on riding, keeps on standing in the fields
of praise to hold onto the faith of roots people.
Brother Solomon, you put the name Ephraim
on your head and carry the face of the true
Rasta, the face of an Ashanti warrior, eyes deep
under heavy lids, and your skin tight as leather,
blacker dan black. I have met you before
on the streets of Kingston, there where you trod
to the hiss and slander of the heathen, you,
natty dread, gathering the people's broken minds
into your calabash. You carry it all, tell them
Return to the roots, the healing shall take place.
You are Burning Spear's voice in the fields of *teff,*

you tell me of the prophecy of Marcus,
and I listen to you, through the phlegm,
through the gruff of your voice, then suddenly
when I ask about the passing of the Emperor,
you rise up like a staff of correction, your voice
reaching back to the mountains, your warrior
self, your yardman greatness, and you speak
a mystery of those who have ears but won't hear,
who have eyes and won't see, and I know
that this dread will one day stand
in this soil, and find his feet growing roots,
that soon the earth will be darker for the arrival
of Solomon. Let the heathen rage, let the doubters
scoff, let this Ghanaian youth whose eyes
have seen the face of Jesus Christ, let him too
sit and marvel at the faith of the natty.
For this African Postman has forsaken
father and mother, and has come to stand
before His Imperial Majesty, to call only him
Father, so that the Father might call him son,
and the world will carry on its weary march,
and the ibises will swoop in the Ethiopian dusk
and the smoke will rise from wood fires,
and the night will come with news that the roots-
man, after four hundred years of being told
he is homeless, has come home, yes, Jah,
has come home.

> *Sons and daughters of His Imperial Majesty Haile Selassie,*
> *Earth Rightful Ruler, without any apology say:*
> *This is the time when I and I and I should come home,*
> *yes, Jah… Nah leggo! Nah leggo! Nah leggo!*
> Winston Rodney

LION

In Wondo Genet, the hot water from the mountains
stings the skin, and steam rises from the slippery
blue-painted baths, and I dip and wade trying
to cleanse myself. I am a fat man in Ethiopia;
they marvel at the columns of my thighs,
the breasts, the pale in my skin – there is no shame
in looking with questions, or in whispering
in rapid Amharic. Above us, the jungle
stretches: dense trees, the flame of colours,
and the sudden dart and disappearing of monkeys.
The women and girls are demure in their two
pieces; they bend their knees as they wade
so they are dragging the water against their breasts.
Ethiopia is a grand spa with rusting railings,
a tarnished gentility, and the youths
smile with questions. I am waiting
for a woman to pass – thin, with her hair
falling in cascades of black grapes
like the beloved in the *Song of Songs*,
her eyes dark lined; the smooth
featureless journey to her lips
before the cheekbones startle you
with their clean line – to move
past me, making her way to the ladder,
when I see tattooed on her back
the imperial lion, one paw held up
holding the *ites*, green and gold flag,
the green lion in perpetual roar
there on her right shoulder blade.
It feels like a secret code,
like an assertion that the Emperor
still lives, hidden under the skin.

REACH

I come in search of diadem and sceptre.
I come in search of a doddering old man.

I come in search of the glory of warrior kings.
I come in search of the burden of patronage.

I come in search of the eyes that burned.
I come in search of the body in the latrine.

I arrive in a city that has expunged a hero
gone to seed – perhaps he stayed too long
or perhaps he has not gone, not quite yet.

I come in search of the conquering lion.
I come in search of the hubris of empire.

I come in search of the ancient faithful.
I come in search of the blasphemy of Rasta.

I hold in me dusty questioning, seeking
out the whisperers and the scoffers.

It is raining in Addis, the air is thin
and I know only that these faces,
these beautiful faces, are the faces
of those uncertain of majesty.

When man is God and God is man,
myth and magic walk hand in hand
with blood and madness and decay.

In this land, it is possible
to hear the voice of God
in the voice of the dead.

LUNCH TIME
For Amtaz Shete

What hurt most was how the city returned to its ordinary routine:
the beggars clustering around the cars, the Grojjan and Tigray traders
hawking their wares and someone laughing a hearty laugh,
as if they, too, had not awoken to see this shadow over us.

The rains arrived at midday and shrouded the day with cold
and the comforts of the familiar – it was easy to pass the palace
without a prayer – the emperor was a wasted old man walking
the paths of power while all the trappings of majesty
fell away – but it was the way of the old, and no blood was spilled;
even the conspirators praised him, fell before him and hailed him;
and God had not stopped the rains. The priests still collected the alms,
repeated the drone of prayer for the saints to welcome the penitent dead.

All was constant in the world, except for this slow drive through the city,
the car smelling of fresh stews and the pungent sour of cool *njera*
(he might have preferred a steak but national food was patriotic
and peasant nationalism the new law).

The guard pushed his hand into the canteen, felt around,
turned over the tidy order of the meal, while we stood
eyes averted, afraid to look, though I could see when he peered
over the shades that he was but a boy, a simple boy giddy with new
power. He licked his fingers, nodded us in, and the meal was silence,
no answers, no promises, just the sound of soft rain falling.

NEW YEAR'S EVE IN ADDIS

Addis is dark at night, as if the low grade
electricity cannot burn through the heavy gloom.

On New Year's Eve, the shops are emptying,
the pavements are covered with the aromatic

green of cut grass, and women sell bundles
of the welcome carpets and dry firewood.

The smoke begins to thicken in the air –
from bonfires with a red glow at each house

and small dwelling. It is hard to breathe
so far up in the highlands; the air is being

purified – all sins, all errors, all wayward acts
burnt away by flame; the smoke clogs the nostrils

with the acrid reminder of failure. The penitents
will bathe in soft rainwater, cover their skin

with palms full of medicated powder, and the bodies
will be robed in gleaming white – the cloth of hope.

In the dim light of pre-dawn, the women follow
the antiphonal groans of the priests at St. Stephens –

the scent of incense can carry for miles in the cool
morning air. They arrive at the courtyard and begin

to press clean lips to the floor of the sanctuary,
to open clean palms and cup the blessings falling

from the crosses' maze of lines. Like women
bathing in a river, they scoop the healing on their

heads, their voices muttering the *Ge-ez* of penitence
until they too can enter the holy place and bow.

The past must enter the blood as ritual – that which
remains is the gold and the precious silver of tradition –

and in this season we learn the theology of forgiveness,
the promise of forgetting all things – the amnesia

of the gospel. It is how a people could forget
the monument of the emperor; how, come Maskal,

the sins of a brutish summer can turn into smoke –
a burning in the eyes, some tears for a while

before the balm of weeping, the cleansing of prayer
and the ordinary rituals of facing new days.

The penitent does not make God; it is God who made
the penitent; it is not for us to know the answers;

questions are for those who have not yet learnt
the insignificance of the short time we are given here.

ROUTINE
Bath, 1936-41

People, like children, find comfort in routine;
children never doubt their people-ness;
they read eyes, test the waters, find comfort
in habit. Two sloping miles along the road,
at a constant pace, with occasional slowing
to view the stretch of farmlands of Bath,
one can predict the moment the soapstone
yellow walls of this enterprising city began
to assert the permanence of industry and craft.
At the post office – one comes to expect the soft
nod of villagers – it takes two weeks for routine
to turn into comfort. Soon they will miss me
when I have found my way back to familiar
roads – the gravel and dust of Addis, the walk
among the robed subjects, my people
bowing low to greet me – these who have long
learnt the comfort of an emperor among them.
For now, it's a smile, a word about the light
or the bite of cold the night before, the same
smile, the same words – people find comfort
in routine. This is the wisdom of kings and queens,
those who have learnt to raise a prostrated
person with ordinary grace, so there is nothing
of shame in the duty of the respectful.
Oh, Jesus, they have taken away everything
you gave me; they have caused me to risk
the abuse of my patriots and warriors
by turning me into a fleeing man. Must not
the emperor be the last to stand,
must he not be willing to fall bleeding
into the earth for the land, for the people,

for the kingdom? Why have you let
my enemies gather about me, leaving me to sing
songs of return in this strange land? Even
an emperor finds comfort in the rituals
of a long promenade through this clockwork
city of polite bows, curious stares, and the grace
of knowing that, after all, an Ethiope does not
have a second head lodged under his arm,
an Ethiope can offer the delicacy of decorum
and polite inconsequential conversation;
an Ethiope can keep time, arrive and depart
from the yellow city of abbeys and halls
with constant precision. They will miss me,
miss the routine of exile, and I, too, will miss
the small comforts of a leisurely royal walk.

ELEGY FOR HEROUY

On September 1940, Herouy a close confident of Emperor Haile Selassie I, died in Fairfield Villa, Bath, England.

Herouy, I walked two miles to Bath in rain;
the Hombourg will keep me from fevers
and a trembling death this winter. I have not
heard the soft tread of your feet at my back
for months; now all I hear is the shadow
of your voice in the soft wind through trees.
I prayed for you in Malvern yesterday –
an owl hooted, like the owls in Wando Genet.
It is still the rainy season in Harar
and the mountainsides will be bright
with the *meskal* daisies of the new year.
There is nothing more desolate than death
in a foreign land. I brought you here
to see you die. We tried to chant the prayers
of our people, so take comfort, friend,
Jesus will speak our language, too.
I could hear him whisper Amharic
in the trees over the Lockwood Cemetery.
I feel naked, now; they have stolen
all we had, and Halifax, as you said,
wears a bwana hat and his mouth is full
of the deceits of colonisers. They want
our holy land, Herouy. Though these obsequious
Bathonians smile, they do so with pity.
An emperor needs justice, not pity;
he needs arms, the flint of resistance
not the milk of pity from peasants.
But these are the gifts we have been given,
and it is no longer your worry, my friend.

I have no friends I can trust any more,
no one who loves me with your simple
obedience and wisdom. I looked back
on the climb up Kelston Road, half-
expecting to see you shuffling, bowed
behind. The road home seems a long way;
we should have died with Italian
sabres in our throats on the streets
of Addis, not here in this mute city.
Forgive me, my friend, for not granting
you the hot, noble death of a patriot;
all I have given is this eating disease
reducing you to a shadow,
huddled in the yellow Bath stone –
like Toussaint, Napoleon, and all
ensnared warriors, weaponless
and impotent as infants. Forgive me,
my brother, my father, my friend.

3

BRIMMING

TYRE AND SIDON

A sudden sun;
the green below us is soft.

We are writing songs
about the colour of light.

The arms of the branches
are twisted. There is a scream

at the edges of the sun
and words like *bomb*,

concussion, *tumult*
and *blood* are hurled

into the red sky.
I trim my lawn today.

Somewhere else, people
cannot rely on the sun;

their skies are thick
with billowing smoke.

DREAMING OF ST. AUGUSTINE

Stono, South Carolina, 1738

At dawn, the mist settles on our skin.
We are sweating through the thick underbrush.
Ahead, light is the ghost of hope;
behind, the darkness is shelter.
We are running south towards the river,
hoping to find the shallow crossing
where the dense forest near the border
is the hope of freedom. We are running
leaving behind the splatter of blood,
the prayers of the saints, the stench
of rum, the howl of dogs, the clamour
of our chains. Savannah River whispers
in the silence. We baptize our faces
with a handful of Spanish moss,
suck the water from its tendrils,
then run, keep running, hoping
for the sound "*St. Augustine*",
for the language we have long
forgotten; for a gentle, gentle sleep.

HOW TO PICK A HANGING TREE

Pastoral scene of the gallant south,
The bulging eyes and the twisted mouth,
Scent of magnolias, sweet and fresh,
Then the sudden smell of burning flesh.
                                        Lewis Allan

Young trees may look sturdy, but they have no memory,
they are green so near the surface they bend with the sudden weight;
and the truth is that not all trees can carry a man's dead weight
with enough air between pointed toes and earth, with enough height
so the scent of rotting can carry far enough to be a message
for those who are sniffing the muggy air for news.

Old as it may look, craggy bark, twisted branches,
drooping limbs, old as it may seem sitting there by the edge
of the canal, that live oak understands the simple rituals of hanging.
See, there is the natural notch where the rope will slip
and hold, and here, angled like this, the damp air
off the river, carries the decay for miles and miles.

Sometimes, a fresh tree will simply die after the piss
of a dying man seeps into its roots. Sometimes a tree
will start to rot from guilt or something like a curse.
But the old trees, seasoned by the flame of summer lightning,
and hardened to tears, know it is nothing to be a tree, mute
and heartless, just strong enough to carry a man until he turns to air.

LOST IN ENOREE COUNTY

Too afraid to admit it, we lied to ourselves
that once the rain had slowed to a dew
we would find the path back.

It has stopped and we sit in the
crowded cave of vines and bramble
staring at the yellow ghost of light.

We are, we know, sitting on the ancient
bed of a long dead river, and ahead
the grotto will lead to an open valley
where a lake once gleamed.

There is no comfort in this. Our map
promises nothing but forest beyond
the storm. So we sit in the shelter,
wiping water from our faces.

Our skin is green and yellow, dappled
with hints of reds. We strip, we say,
to dry our clothes, but that is another lie.

Ours is the ritual of burial — as if
after our orgasm we will lay here
and become lumps of earth, moss-
covered bones, green, red, and yellow
as the underbelly of this jungle.

BRIMMING

A silken veil, this light rain
softens the flaming oak leaves.

The Tarmac is gleaming wet.
Gold on the black river's belly.

Deep at night, the rain lifts;
a cool breeze tickles my skin,

dries sweat and the dew's mist.
Naked, I slip through the woods.

A new fist of cloud crowds the west;
I stand, head back and open-mouthed.

GONE FISHING

There's your hoe out in the sun
Where you left a row half done...
                    Louis Armstrong and Bing Crosby

Catfish, bream and red-eye bass,
river of muscadines, of hardwood
bluffs, and mossy grottoes,
here in the soft piedmont
earth is where I come
to rest, where the shelter
of green crowds away
the memory of wide open
spaces, deserts, blood
in sand, the dry stench
of rotting bodies, the voice
of the leader edged
with jest and the boast
of a barroom brawler,
brittle bramble on waterless
plains, the ache in me
for my dead brother,
for the shattered limbs,
for the ordinary order
of the suburbs where
the world is oblivious
to the sound that prophets
make when they wail
across a city trembling
with the falling of bombs.
I toss an arc of black net
so it falls tenderly
on the olive-yellow surface

of the whispering river;
then I wait in the ticking
heat for the weight
of the catch, then I pull
with the slow grunting
of a labourer, consumed
by his labour, knowing
only that the hum of trees
will not be startled
by sudden explosions,
but will fall asleep
at thickening dusk.

RIVER LOVE

Grey summer dawn light,
their caught breath shivers the air —
the taste of sweet lime.

She is counting now
the tremors of his body
at each sharp lightning flash.

Her tongue tutors him
in the pull and suck of mud.
He rises for breath.

How to hold her up
while she brings the heavy sky
down on him wetly.

Above, the ash clouds
gather quickly, murmuring
across the spring sky.

The brackish water
is where their mouths meet: her salt,
his fresh stream, mingling.

GRAVES

After the light-coloured shallows,
the deep river is our resting place.

We plunge into the chill;
everything is black down here.

Staring upwards, the sky
glows in mists of green and silver.

Below the river bed undulates
like a drought-burnt prairie.

Deeper, the smooth shoulder
of a sudden valley glows yellow.

We find the skulls of simple folk
buried in the broken graveyard

on the slopes of a village
lost to the floodwaters of a trained

river; we find a brick crucifix,
and the sound of prayers murmuring

in the dark belly of this river.
When we come up for air

the boat has drifted far down-
stream, and a soft rain is falling.

PEACH WINE AND POLITICAL POETRY
for Sheila Tombe

Sheila is searching for political poems;
she is sure they no longer exist. I send her
a poem thick with metaphors – something
by David, the New York poet who recites
Langston Hughes poems in quaint soirées
where old yellow women remember themselves
as flamboyant dancers in Harlem clubs
so many years ago when poems *were*
political, and poets were committed,
and those who were not got syphilis
and died sad deaths. They are, of course,
half drunk on peach wine, and half
giddy with their fading brains, so David
is a hit till he reads *his* poems
which are, he promises, intimations
on green – lime, croton, pond, elm
in spring, and the impossible palette
of a Caribbean valley at dusk before
the ordering of cane-fields, before
the island was turned from rain forest
to plains and valleys by the discipline
of tobacco groves. He describes
a thin oblique circle of bone and straw
reflecting, like a looking glass,
a sky of mountainous greens
overlapping like clouds of storm.
Half the women have fallen asleep,
the other half wrapped in lime-green
scarves are complaining of hunger
and dancing around the room.
Sheila will not publish David's

poem. *Too literal*, she says,
and he has not understood
the politics of memory and forgetting
or the meaning of green.
Anyway, at no point does he
mention Bush. Those women
told him as much when they asked for
more wine, and he said he had to go.

SHELTER

He hideth my soul in the cleft of the rock
that shadows a dry thirsty land
                                    Fanny J. Crosby

A shelter without windows
or cracks in the walls

is a lie. We must see
the flaming red sky

of the Second Coming
to know we have found

peace in the cleft
of the rock. A man

stammering prayers
with his face covered

must see the heat of God
through his glowing fingers.

ON LANDSCAPE PAINTING AND PIONEERS

How easily we find thighs
in open landscapes, the smooth
slopes of mountains, the deep
darkness of river valleys
where we paint a purplish
mist of gauze as if to cover
the flow of musky water;
how easily we find
ourselves on the edge
of a wide terrain, peering
through the sinewy limbs
of unruly trees, standing
like a veil between us
and the rich colour of the world
we will enter, plant our flag
and name. How easily
our gaze settles on thighs,
on wide open skies,
on hints of rain in the distance
as if we arrived here first,
as if no one parted
these hanging vines
before we arrived with our
canvasses, palettes and paints.

CAROLINA GOLD

for Brian Rutenberg

Hurl me through memory
and I will return panting
with my satchel filled
with the stories strangers
tell me at the crossroads.

In the low country
it takes just a few years
for a storm's scars to heal,
for the moss and thickets
to cover crumbled stones.

In the low country
a forest covers a multitude
of sins, and we make camp
humming, trying not to hear
the clamour underfoot.

If you walk barefoot
through the forest, you will
feel the dip and swell
of old graves, how near
the surface is the water table.

Words like "beauty"
are the artist's hope, but
his dreams are of terror
and the testing of light –
the language of colour.

I walk through this hall
and find myself tossed
from light to light,
and it is hard to breathe,
hard to stop to look.

Outside, the sudden light
of Columbia in July
is strange comfort.
I make blood poems
before I sleep.

STONO

After Mark Smith

I: Blessings

July's confession

They call me July cause my skin eats heat.
Lost my other name so long ago
it don't mean nothing. Gave me shoes for my feet,
a red coat with brass buttons, and a fat cow
cause I killed a man, killed that slave boy, Luke.
Drunk on liquor he stole down by Stono –
killed him just cause he wouldn't take rebuke
from me. Dumb "Angolan", kills his owner
and stead of running, stops to dance and drink
until old Bull returned with sixty men
hungry for blood. Well, I know how to think,
know how to work things out, know an omen
from a blessing, and Luke's head was my blessing.
Break it now, get some clothes – work it out in heaven.

II: The Butcher

How can I face such slaughter and be cool?
                              – Derek Walcott

We'll break them now, then work it out in heaven
where old Cato will see what he's been dreaming
all these years: the pink white of a dogwood season;
the sharp blue of a low country sky screaming
with hawks; the crimson sheet over his face
before everything went black. That sweet day

100

he will sing old Kongo hymns and taste grace.
Old Cato knows how to pick cotton and pray
for cool breeze on his wet back: "Wake at dawn,
Lord, toil till darkness come, that's how they do
us Africans." Cato keep singing songs,
smiling always at the red, white and blue
faces of Mass Lemy and his bitch wife
split in two by his swinging butcher knife.

III: Inspire

Jemmy's prayer

Split them in two with your swinging butcher knife,
it's Mother Virgin Mary's birthing day.
Come Sunday morning, we will all arrive
at the field by Pons Pons, kneel and pray,
then filled with grace, break the flesh, drink the blood,
and appease the dead warriors buried
under an ocean of woes. Who said God
had forgotten us? Who said Mother Mary
does not walk with us? The heat is thick
this September morning – I can smell
the swelling flesh of Godfrey and his sick-
headed son – twelve and already knows well
the sweetness of gutting a man to death.
Yes, how I love that warm taste on my breath.

IV: Rally

Cato rallies the troops

Yes, I love that warm taste on my breath,
the salt and iron of a broken tongue,
the smell of blood libations in the earth
among a silk cotton's roots spread around,
the stink of new sweat flowing from my skin,
not from hauling wood or picking cotton
but from what each warrior muscle was trained
to do: swing machete, crack some bones,
fire a musket, rush the enemy,
dance around the fire, dance and sing,
just because man is man and must be free
to walk this earth without no chains
on his feet, scars on his back, no auction block;
today we catch back [our] breath while we take stock.

IV: Biding Time

Cato's Wife

So man must catch back breath while he take stock
of every wound [hurt] his body has been taking.
All the long night he wake with staring shock
in his eyes, his body tense and shaking;
mumbling that funny talk like that white man
who come slinking behind the row of trees
by the river where the two of them stand
and talk. They was hatching plots in the privy,
smelling of all that shit and piss, and as
day pass day, he growing tenser until

102

he had to tell me, had to get release.
Man is like that, they always have to spill
their guts, but a woman like me can hold
it, waiting for the right time to explode.

VI: *Herbalist*

"Unsex me here..." Lady Macbeth

Cato's Wife

Hold it in for the right time to explode,
then you must let the blood rush to your head,
force yourself to grow blind, forget the hold
that mercy has on you. Make all things red:
pillows, bed-sheets, polished floors, curtains;
an infant's cry is the same as the bleat
of goats; grow deaf, toss off every burden
of regret and remorse and let the heat
of battle consume you. And while you
shake, I will crush dry herbs on a wet stone
to feed Old Crawford and his cracker crew
come Sunday, and for days their rotting bones
will ache, their eyes will blister as they see
the end of all they've done to you and me.

VII: Crossing the River

The end of all they've done to you and me
is what we'll find in the slow dark Savannah,
whispering secrets amongst the roots of trees
muscular like a man's hot temper,
waiting to wrap around careless bodies
that have wandered this way at night.
Throw me a stone to confound mysteries;
for one instant the sky broke open and light
streamed down like a miracle. We thought
then it was possible. We could taste it
in our mouths: *Freedom*! We were caught
in our hope, a dream carved with a hatchet.
Coming so close, I wished I had died,
to let me cross over to the other side.

VIII: Florida

To let me cross over to the other side,
I made pacts with these Irish Catholics,
white niggers with leather-tough hides
bitter wit, thick laughter and the tricks
beaten-down folks know like second nature.
Florida is like the promised land for folk
who knew the cleansing of holy incense
and the soothing and tender loving strokes
of Mary. Florida, that grand offence
to Protestant England and Carolina,
that place of legend where man runs free,
stands tall, knows the grace of open skies.
St. Augustine sure ain't no Africa,
but it's heaven after Carolina.

IX: Poles

But it's heaven after Carolina
is done with you. I mean anything must
after this thick stew of choking summers
when you wish for the mercy of dust-to-dust.
On that Monday morning, no sickle cut
through the high rice paddies, no fish-net sailed
to land soft on the open pond, no hot
anvil rang out in the air, no field cook wailed
the call for lunch. We all sat there
in our cabins waiting to be called out
at dusk to watch our men kick out, then stare
dumb, hanging from the oaks. Then they shout
for axes to chop off and poles to plant
their heads as food for flies, for crows, for ants.

X: Coda

Planted on poles for flies, for crows, for ants,
their heads with thick clumps of hair and dried blood –
I know those faces. I have heard the chants
the women make, their tears under the hood
of cast-down eyes. "He who fights and runs away
lives to fight another day." Ah, guerrilla!
I have carried this lie in me always
to ease my shame. I feel the old tremor
in my chest as I stand in Stono field,
the traffic humming through pecan trees.
With no monuments, nothing to make real
these Africans who thought they could see
the shape of huts at dusk, how can I turn,
how can I run away from this dark storm?

XI: I Ain't Free

How can I run away from this dark storm,
this casual brutality, this simple
act of bloodletting as if no great harm
has been done, as if these corporeal temples
mean nothing, count for nothing, as if
something does not break in us when
we learn to picnic around the stiff
grotesquerie of maggot-riddled skin?
A slave, slippery in her birthing waters,
sings, "Take my baby home, take my baby
home, I ain't free," her heart growing harder
for what she has seen, for what she will see,
for what her baby must not see – the years
of bloodshed, the whippings and the tears.

XII: Monument

The blood we shed, the whippings and the tears
cannot be the only stories we must tell
in the dumb silence of these peaceful years
long after slavery's bedlam, Jim Crow's hell,
and the fickle truce we've made with history;
cannot be enough without monuments
planted in the forests where we buried
our restless kin, where we still hear laments
twisting through the entanglement of trees,
the songs of battle, the drums, the fluttering
banners, the hushed suspiration of leaves.
I offer this poem's harnessed stuttering,
architecture from that other nation,
containing our righteous indignation.

NEW DAY

For Barak Obama

I: Obama, January 1st, 2009

Already a halo of grey covers his close-cropped head –
before, we could see the skin-pale glow of his skull, the way
he kept it close – sign that he spends little time in bed;
long hours spent filing things in boxes, colour-coded trays,
calculating the price of expectation – things promised,
all eyes now on him: the winning politician's burden.
On the day he makes his inaugural speech he will miss
the barber shop, the quick smoke in the alley, the poem
found in the remainder box, or just a chance to shoot
some hoops, and those empty moments to remember
the green rice paddy where he used to sprint, a barefoot
screaming boy, all legs, going home to the pure
truth of an ordinary life, that simple place where, fatherless,
he found comfort in the wisdom of old broken soldiers.

II: How Legends Begin

This is how legends begin – the knife slitting the throat
of a hen, the blood, the casual pragmatism of eating
livestock you've fed for months; the myth of a father, a boat
ride into the jungle, a tongue curling, then flinging
back a language alien as his skin; the rituals
of finding the middle ground: navigating a mother's
mistakes, a father's silence, a world's trivial
divisions, the meaning of colour. Now nation-negotiator
of calm, the boy tutored in the arts of profitable charm.
This is how legends begin and we will narrate this, too,
to the children lined up with flags despite the storms
gathering, children who will believe in the hope of blue
skies stretched behind the lowering mountainscape of clouds;
will hear him burnishing language to soothe the teeming crowds.

III: Waking Up American, November 5, 2008

She says she never saw him as black, unlike his mother,
who said she did. Madelyn says she saw him as colourless,
just a man – unlike his white mother who touched his father's
glowing face, the shade of deep brown earth. Grandma says it's best
to see him as just a human in this country that washed
out long ago the pernicious stain of race, and I
call her a tenderhearted dreamer, an unabashed
sweet white-lie teller who would rather tell this bland lie
than admit that she was scared when she walked down King Street
the morning after the nation's votes were counted, she was
frightened, but proud, so giddy with the thumping wild beat
of her heart, knowing that her country made common cause
for a magic instant and did something grand, made a black
man president. Such a miracle, such a sweet soul track.

IV: Punch-line

I've asked this question of them year after year, a punch-line
challenge, primed to go off with clockwork consistency:
Raise your hand if you can truly remember a time
you believed that even you could take the presidency –
yes – blacks, native peoples, women, Latinos – was it when
you were four, five, six? And the suckered believers all
would raise their hands. So the trickery of the second question:
How many of you now suppose you have the wherewithal
to be the chief today? And up go four foolhardy hands:
a dreamer, a liar, a clown, a madman. What went wrong?
How did you all mess up? It's messed up now, the chance is gone
now that a black man's done it! Cancel the class! Time to hang
a poor joke. But we can't complain bout oppression no more;
got to recalibrate who the man is now, that's for sure

V: Palmetto

Of course, our homeland has kept its old promise to itself –
the one that made Eartha, Chubby Checker, Althea Gibson
and James Brown all pack their travelling bags, clean out their shelves,
never to look back South, not once. They created their new songs,
clean slates, like people who've forgotten where their navel-strings
were buried. We kept the promise that made those who stayed learn
to fight with the arts of silence, the subterfuge of rings
of secret flames held close to the heart, kindling the slow burn
of resistance. But good news, despite the final state count,
Columbians know the upheaval of all things brought grace
here where the pine trees bleed and palmettos suck up the brunt
of blows, and so we too can now hum the quiet solace
of victory with a surreptitious shuffle, quickstep
for you, Smoking Joe, Dizzy, James, and Jesse, slide, slide, now step.

VI: Confession

Here is my confession, then, the one I keep inside me:
while the crowds gather in Washington, I will admit this:
it is enough it happened, more than enough that we see
him standing there shattering our excuses; no, not bliss,
not some balm over the wounds that still hurt, but it's enough
to say that we saw it happen, the thing we thought wouldn't
happen, and even feared if it did. Knowing that is tough,
yes, but it is good and grand, beautiful and new, couldn't
wish for more, no matter what comes next, that a man who's kin,
who knows the Chicago blues, knows the stop-time of be-bop,
who's questioned from inside out the meaning of blood and skin,
is, let's just say it, standing there, yes, standing at the top
of the world – it's enough for tomorrow; and yes he's tough
and yes he's smart, but mostly it's sweet and more than enough.

VII: On Having a Cool President

He will not be the buffoon and clown; he's too cool for that.
His cool is the art of ease, the way we drain out tension,
make the hard look easy, with the nonchalance of a cat.
Cool's hiding the burn in the fluid grace of execution.
Cool's knowing how to lean back and let the low punches come –
always ready for them to come. He'll be no minstrel show,
but one who shows, in the midst of chaos, unruffled calm.
Like, what-does-he-think-he-knows-that-we-don't-already-know?
Like, I can be brighter-than-you-and-still-be-way-down cool.
Like some presidential cool – a cool that hasn't much been seen
in the White House before. You see, he's a nobody's-fool
kind of cool, the one that makes a gangsta-lean-look-so-clean
kind of cool. That's what we have now, and I'm truly impressed,
you can call this cool if you want to; me, I call it blessed.

VIII: Lincoln, January 1st, 1863

I think of that other Illinois man, pacing the boards
of a musty mansion, a nation's future in his head,
the continuing concussion of guns, the bloody hordes
of rebels like ghouls in his dreams. He, too, avoids his bed.
Tomorrow the hundred days will be over: four million
souls to be freed; four million lots of property pilfered;
four million free labourers worth their weight in bullion
promised a new day; four hundred thousand owners outraged;
a million looming calamities, all at the flow of ink
from his pen. This is the path of the pragmatist who would
be saviour, the simple act of war, the act to sink
an enemy. Will the hallelujahs break out like loud
ululations of freedom? Uneasy lies the head… who knows?
This is how our leaders are born, how we find our heroes.

4

THUNDER IN THE EGG

You can cut me
Weed me out throw me away
You can burn me
Make charcoal of me
Birds won't stop
Making nests in my roots
Hope won't stop
Blossoming in my heart
I'm a poet
My roots don't have an end

— Emmanuel Eugene

POVERTY

This rusting empty can – I brought soil
from Jérémie and filled it, then I planted
seeds, and waited for them to break open.

Even here in Port-au-Prince, the poet will find
fertile soil for the seeds tied up in her scarf.

There is something beautiful about these gnarled
branches that reach upwards like the songs
of a blind soldier by the roadside.

TOMBS

all day long I watch over a town
that's broken down
            – Josaphat Robert Large

Every crumbled building is a tomb.
We step over grey, crushed bricks
and the entanglement of steel.

The faint scent of death hangs in the air;
every sliver of laughter dries in the heat,
the dust, the stones, the dust, the stones.

The doctor offers a wry smile,
shrugs his shoulders and says,
"C'est la vie, ki pa – la vie ça est terib."

He points to the grey slabs of cement
where the hospital once stood;
he counts eighteen – the women

in maternity with their new babies
and their families counting fingers
and toes – they were on the second floor;

on the first were the diligent nurses;
at the top were the broken bodies
of the healing: they are all entombed

in the stone. For days the scent
of their rotting blanketed our skins;
now, after the blue-helmeted soldiers

sprayed the ruins (they had done
this before) it is bearable – death
sulks in the corner, like our hearts

which leap at each sound of rumbling.
The city dances to live, the music
leaping against despair; an old

woman skips to avoid a truck.
This earth devours the dead
with such efficiency; we are left

with our heads covered in dust,
our eyes searching for familiar
faces, our hearts safely tucked away.

BOY IN BLUE

His voice is licked
but his dreams
are the artillery of words loaded
to uncoil our strength.
— Michel-Ange Hyppolite

The words cluster behind your teeth;
close in, the smooth patina, deep brown,
of your face is alight with the effort:
a boy carrying the weight
of an old man, this body of yours
broken again and again by the accident
of your birth. I follow the slow
wave of your thick lashes; you are
counting the words, searching
your heart for the right music.
"Sometimes, I wonder why,
sometimes I wonder if
my mother did this, then I grow
dark, the world swallows light
around me, then I cry — only
sometimes I cry, and then I laugh;
just like that, in a few seconds,
I laugh and I cry and I dream again.
The drum's sound and fire-tongues
dancing beneath the low rafters
would be easier — a prophet speaking,
explaining why this earth moves,
why so much rubble in our city; even the priest
with his soft, horse eyes, his mouth
moving quickly over my skin, even
that would be easier than this

silence; the dark streets of the city,
the heat in my skin, my mother
praying in the shadows, singing
from deeper than I will ever go.
When I sing, I know how
to fly, and how to reach where
the water eases the spinning
in my stomach, and this blood
is not my enemy when I sing."
We leave you in the growing dusk.
The scent of rain is heavy in the air.
Somewhere beside the broken palace
the sky opens up, and the streets
flood – the sound of cataclysms,
so normal now. I imagine you,
like these children, dancing
in the deluge, naked as holiness.

RETRIBUTION

Though hungry, the body knows the pulsing
of desire – the broken taboo, the secrets;

the lies we offer; the justifications shaped
by anger, hurt, regret; the sweetness of orgasms

and tears; a woman whose perm has washed out,
who can't afford the money to do it right,

who lets her neighbour cover her head
with a concoction of cow brains, olive oil,

yeast, boiled up, because for the first time
in a long time, she wants to be beautiful

for the man who holds her face in his hands
and drags his heavy lips over her skin.

How she has cried for the betrayal and niceness,
how she has trembled on her walk through

the streets deep in the night, knowing
that God will plant a knife at the corner

to bring shame to her family – as if shame
could come even more – the fear that soon

he will tell her that he is sick, too, and then
she will have to say that she has been sick

and has been afraid to tell him of her sickness
for fear he would stop loving her, and how

she calculated that the blow he would land
on her shoulders with his machete, and the blade

he would plant in her stomach are far
better than the emptiness she would feel

ending it with him, walking away from him,
going hungry, not just for a meal, but for love.

This is how our secrets undo us; this is how
this city becomes all cities; how this small world

is all worlds; how a skirt is a skirt; how blood
is blood; how the moon is fat over the cathedral

at night – a woman thankful for its light,
her thighs bruised with exertion, her stomach

full of the turmoil of being filled as if for the first
time in the small shack in the city of laments.

DOLORS ATRAVÈ

To get to the clinic the bus costs too much,
counting my gourdes for tomorrow's milk –
the healing of milk, milk to make me fat,
the light in milk, the soft thickness

of milk, the silk of milk, the tenderizing
of milk making everything in me clean,
turning the black shadow of these days
into something of brightness. One day

I said, "My blood is black" and my mother
said, "Don't say black like it is a curse" –
she used to march and sing songs about
Toussaint, and she is right, but my blood

is black, thick like tar. If I bleed it will
be black – not like my skin, though
these days I wonder if my skin, too,
has not betrayed me, like my hair.

I asked her to cut it like Michael Jackson's
and she laughed and said, "My singer, you
can't move like Michael Jackson," and she
is right, I can't move, though I am all

bones like him, and sometimes
when I watch him walk, he is unsteady
like I am, walking to the clinic, to the hand
holding out pills, to the interrogation

of the caring people – the ones who
manage what they promise is our shelter.
So many times I have been told that I, too,
might be dead like they used to die

before they got the pill – and I want to
be grateful like they want me to be;
I want to be one of the Lazarus people,
but mostly I think of Michael and his money,

and how in a crowd, in his pajamas,
he looks so tired, like I feel walking
into the secret society of the broken.
Nobody has said he, too, does not have

black blood, so I am not a liar to think
he does. The road to the clinic is always
melting, the rubble clogging the pathways;
I wobble over the bricks and cement;

I should be sweating, but I have no sweat
to give. I cover my mouth to keep out
the dust and sometimes the stench
of the dead that leads to the clinic –

it will take too many gourdes to catch
a bus to the clinic, so I walk,
the dust covering my shoes white. Sometimes
I sing in my head, moving through the crowd

like Jesus on the stony path to the hill,
the crowd pressing in – like Michael in his
pajama pants, walking towards the light
as if he is dead. The gawking crowds cannot

see the smile inside of him, and they can't
hear the music in his stomach, or the milk
circling in his blood. This is my body,
this is my head heavy at noon, blood weary;

this is my body, waves of heat rushing
up the bottom of my spine; these are
my hands; these are the hands of a broken
man; this is my body, this is my dancing body.

EAVESDROPPING

I fear our bodies are so crowded
in this city of a million crossroads

that our neighbours will hear my dreams,
know my secret, the one I have hidden

for years in my blood. At night I pray,
whispering, *God, dry up my dreams*.

SENSE

In the land of Haiti
kids are dreaming
but they only dream nightmares.
They see snakes that are crawling
with little cups of water 'round their necks.
— Georges Castera

1

Our trauma teaches us how to hear
the rumble of a truck hurtling
through the city of potholes
and broken bricks; the shudder —
we know the sound of the ground
mumbling — hungry, always hungry.

2

Our trauma teaches us how to see,
every edifice, each storey a calculation
of survival. Nothing lasts forever,
the standing things must soon
be laid low, the solid turned
to the pulverized dust of loss;
I enter each building, eyes pulsing.

3

Our trauma teaches us how to smell
the scent of honeysuckle and lavender,
the pungence of ripe mangoes, the dull
stench of sewers, stagnant for days,
the sweet rot of old garbage, soaked
by rain, then steaming, the rank
of urine staining the cracked walls,
the hum of bodies still buried
under the stones – a faint decay
we grow used to. Why we spit and then
cross ourselves as we pass by.

4

Our trauma teaches us how to feel
the warm flesh we hold, the living
still with us, the grace of bodies
touching, the rough grit of concrete
blocks we lift and lift, pushing past
the chaos, trying to find what has been
lost, what we have not touched for months,
pushing past the hard caging of steel
and stone, seeking out the soft give
of fingers beneath the stone, the caress
of cloth, the wetness of flesh.

5

Our trauma teaches us how to taste
the salt in our sweat,
the salt in our tears, the salt in our blood.
These days when we fuck, we lick
our faces and fingers – we want to taste
what it is to bleed and sweat; we taste
the funk in our skins, the musk
on our tongues, the salt on cracked
lips, the long kiss, the salt in the evening
air down by the sea's edge, the salt
of dust rising, the salt in our cocoa,
the salt in the dust lifting from the ruins;
and then the sweet news of stewed
garden eggs, the surprise of honey,
the taste of the air cool at evening time,
the darkness coming quicker than normal,
the clouds gathering over Port au-Prince
rushing across the shelter of the mountains,
the sweetness of the sudden rain on our skins.

BARON SAMEDI

Here death has become
an acquaintance,
the quick face staring
at the corner in Carrefour,
the mute gaze of passengers
bouncing in the casket
of a bus with its hieroglyphs
of prophecy and blessing.
It is familiar, of course;
we transplanted Africans
crowd these new cities,
grow numb from our labours,
and at day's end are
dumb corpses going
home. I have long known
how work has undone
so many. Death is the stone
eyes of a woman selling
mangoes, behind her eyes
a universe of catastrophes,
things so absurd, so ridiculous:
in a week the eviction notice,
the dead cousin, the dead uncle,
the slip of paper with the word
positive, the pregnant daughter –
not the whore, but the one who
read her books and sat
under the trees in the backyard
unguarded, the job lost,
and then the earthquake.
She has escaped the falling

birds – a curse placed by a priest.
They did fall, forty of them,
in the yard, and though shocked,
she acted quickly so that by
mid-morning the yard was cleared,
save for a few black and grey
feathers, save for the smell
of tobacco and rum in the air.
Did you smell it?
Here death is a simple prayer,
and the ravaging of all that is
beautiful, all that is giddily alive,
is the secret a nation
of the broken can hold.

Celeste, while cleaning
the rooms, got the call
on her cell, so she sat
down afterwards hoping
to stop the spinning of her head.
She decided to have a smoke,
and to sip from her thermos
some old rum she used to cool
her skin, though these days
she drinks it in small sips,
so that by three o'clock
she is sleepy and pleasant,
singing lewd songs
as she mops the red-tiled
corridors, flooding the area
with too much water. That room –
B98 – where she heard it,
she cannot forget; it always smells

heavy with death, which is why
she turned the painting
in the room upside down
to reverse the curse. No one
has moved it since. It has been
three years. This, like all
the calamities of her life,
she will take with her to the grave.
Here death is a woman's
soft snore late into the night –
her daughter with her baby in her
making her grow a beard,
making her snore; the absence
of the voice we expect to say,
"It is well." Well, it is not well,
not here in this city where Job
is the patron saint of hope,
as the Baron's cottoned nose bleeds,
as he skanks through the streets.

THE VISITOR

He came the night of the 2006
      World Cup Finals, rubbing his forehead
and giggling: "Those Algerians," he said.
      His French was impeccable, though
when the last whistle blew he cursed like a fisherman
      from Cap Haitien. The demon sat
in the backyard on the broken desk we had been
      using for kindling when the gas was out.
He told me my yard was too small;
      people, he said, could see him from the street,
so I built a fence with some rusted
      zinc sheets I found in the abandoned
construction site where the Americans
      had begun a garment factory, before
they gave up and fled because of the blood
      in the lanes. The demon liked
the fence, which was good, but he ate too
      much. He ate everything I had
and if he hated my food, which sometimes
      he did, he would vomit it out
right there in the yard and demand water
      and mints and another meal. I knew
enough to give him what he wanted. He
      was not a pleasant man, and not
quite what I expected: he hated sex for one,
      and felt that parties and dances
were a waste of time. All he did was gossip,
      and he knew everything evil and twisted
about everyone who walked by. I was startled,
      for he knew things about the most

innocent of women that I had not known,
        and though I feigned indifference
as he talked, he knew I relished his gossip,
        especially because of the detail
of what he knew – not so much what people
        said in the open, but things they
thought; and he traded in filth, so much
        of it, so much of it. He sulked
a lot. At nights he stood and shook
        his wings, "dusting off", he said,
which was another insult about my yard.
        But I sat with the demon most
evenings just to hear him talk, and maybe
        I knew that if he spoke to me,
he would have no one else to tell my secret
        thoughts to, and I knew he knew
my thoughts, even though I tried hard
        to be so pure in my dreams day and night.
So I took comfort in the way he let me
        sit and talk with him, since he knew
that I was lonely and sometimes pathetic,
        and that did not bother him, and he
never said anything about that side of me,
        though he could have. Everyone had
gone – my lover took his machete
        and all his clothes, and left; when
I'd offered him half of the plates and cups
        and knives and forks and spoons, he spat
and walked away. He did not even have
        the courtesy to say "No thanks".
I told the demon about this, and he said,
        "What to do?" because he knew,
and maybe he felt it was my fault, and that
        is what we say when we don't want

to say things that might hurt people. He
        did not seem to mind my crying – maybe
he did not care – but when you have lived
        what I have lived, that is like caring –
really. We would sit under the mango
        tree all day and the tree stopped
bearing fruit even though all the trees
        in the neighbourhood had the biggest crop
I have ever seen, and the whole street smelt
        sweet with rotten fruit and worms.
One day I ran out of food, and the demon
        said he was tired of this, and he left.
Just like that. He picked up his stuff,
        walked across the dusty yard, through
the gap in the fence, and was gone. The next
        day it was cooler than usual, and then
the earth shook and my fence fell flat
        on the ground, and when you looked
the broken house was like an island on a metal-
        blue sea tinted with blood.

DEW

This morning I took the dew from the broad
leaf of the breadfruit tree, and washed

the sleep from my eyes. I saw a blue
sky. The cock crowed again and again.

On such mornings, each deep breath,
clean as new light, is a blessed gift.

JOB

For Joel Sainton

This is a home,
this is a shelter,
these are walls, shaken,
these are lines of jagged
cracks, the split
at the ceiling
that lets in light
and rain: this is
my comfort, here,
deep in the catacombs
of Port-au-Prince,
shaded by a giant
breadfruit tree
with its fragile
branches, its bounty;
here where the yard
is cluttered with trash,
trying leaves, and
broken bricks
salvaged from the ruins,
dumped here for use
later, they keep saying –
they being those searching
through the broken
houses for paper
and, in truth,
for money, bread, pots,
clothes and an answer
to our calling of her
name. This is home
where I pray each
night: "Teach me

the calculus of Job,
teach me the madness
of Hosea, teach me
how to be a priest
of suffering, teach
me how to gamble
your name for my gain,
teach me to dream of open skies,
air clear as creek
water for these ravaged
lungs, fruit to flesh
out these bones
under my beaten skin,
sugar to make me fat.
May you wake me
before the next
cataclysm, that I
might rise and leave
this place before
it, too, collapses
like all things have.
Teach me how
to sleep deeply
with the faith that
you will wake me
when it is time. Teach
me to sleep, with no
hope of rising under
this cracked shelter;
teach me, man,
listless like this, blood-
sick like this, shunned
like this, teach me
the way of Job;
teach me."

ABOUT BEANS AND SHIT

The doctor asked me why I did this to her,
asked me why I put her through all of this;
and she clucked her tongue, and ministered

to my wife, who sat silently, her eyes sunken
deep, her whole soul weak with sorrow.

Was I wrong to say, "Doctor, it is the person
who eats beans that will shit beans."? I said it
like Jesus, and I hoped the doctor would see

the crown of thorns twisted around my head.
"Christ is my new wife now," I said, as she
cleaned the yeast from my wife's broken mouth.

SILENCE

In our silence we imagine
the shield of mercy as if
love's impossible good fortune
will keep the wolf from
the door. Here is how
we count our risks and
the mercies of God: this
half of an island, this
claw of a crab, this
city sheltered by mountains,
this scattering of quick
edifices, the disorder
of improvised lives here
where the pink cathedral
overlooks the squalor,
and saints cross themselves
at each flattened building,
at each broken chapel,
at each quickly erected
crucifix where a church
once stood. Here
we count our tragedies:
the dead, the disinterred,
the lost; the infants
secreted into the shadow
of orphanages, or bundled
off in Nike sweats across
the hills, then the sea;
the world between home
and namelessness; the sound
of madness breaking
through the night.

Here, where even the dogs
have fled or have been
crushed by falling stones,
a woman can be forgiven
for saying she has had
enough. So imagine
that in this sweetness
of a man pouring his need
into her – in this instance
when everything depends
on her, when his mind is
hers to flame or extinguish,
when nothing else matters,
in this tender flight
from the burden of finding
the next meal – here
hunger leaves the sweet
dizziness that makes
her orgasm an alarming
act of grace. This free
gift, this respite, this mercy,
this balm: who can blame
her for the way she shouted
into the night? It is
her burden now, not just
the guilt of his stumble
into fatigue and inertia,
but the questions she can't
answer, the ones he asks
her from her gate – not
the weight of his anger
and his tears, not his silence,
the resignation, and the hand
he placed on her hand,

the soft sigh of acceptance.
Oh Haiti, who is watching
to see when the burden
becomes too much;
when will they say,
stop, enough, enough?

STORM

For Malia Jean

From here the mountains around
Port-au-Prince are green. Too
far to see the denuded hillsides,
too far to see the brown wounds,
too far to see the layered
city of sand bags, wooden
reinforcements, heavy plastic
tents, the gravel, the dust,
the narrow lanes, the gutters,
the stolen power lines,
the makeshift clubs, the cinema,
the internet café, the phalanx
of shower booths, the admonitions
to keep the place clean — as if
someone hopes to restore
this stripped-down hillside
to its glory as a golf course.
Too far to see the constant cloud
from wood fires and coal
factories tucked into this
city of improvisation. Too far,
though from here you can smell
the rain gathering at dusk,
the deluge that tonight will heal
all sores, clear the air of dust
from the crushed stones.
Tonight the alabaster ruins
will gleam through the tender
mist of rain, and this body
that has grown weary with living
will hope for a flame of prophesy,

for even the smallest ember,
to keep the heat from slipping
away. This is my world
these days, this and the ritual
of pills, the cycle of nausea,
the relief at three in the afternoon,
the hour when I feel as normal
as I was before all of this —
the blackness at the edge
of my eyes returns by five.
Here is where my prayers
are stripped of all ostentation;
here faith is tasteless
as unleavened bread; here
hope is a whisper from a dried
mouth, and I know what
the presence of God is.
The cool silence of a cemetery
at twilight is my comfort.
I long to make a deal with God:
take this body; it is used up now;
let it rest, dear God, let it
rest. Take this body, it is
yours now, let it rest, Lord,
let it rest. The storm covers
the earth; I stand in the rain.
It comes like the sound of grace,
soaking me to the bone: first
the taste of salt, then the clean
flow of healing slipping in my mouth.

AFTER THE EARTHQUAKE

At night, though the streets
are barren, and the traffic

has slowed down, everything
seems close, and a crowd

fills the air, breathing,
shuffling, moving in the shadows.

My skin prickles, brushed by soft fabric.

PRAYERS

I: Thanksgiving

Oh Christ, who stands on the outer edge
of the broken cathedral with its pink
walls turned to dust, I must look up
to you; you, hovering over this city
of stones and tents. It is like
that other time you wept over
a city, called out her name as if
she was your child. They say you
are Catholic, but it is all the same
to me. My lips move, I speak,
and my words carry over the din
of the city resurrecting itself.
I came here before catching
the bus out of the city into
the green village, just to hear you say
that tomorrow is not promised,
and I need you to know
that I have prayed for a basket
of fresh garden eggs to give
to Celeste, who you know is dying,
who loves their the slippery
sweetness. And you gave me
a cheap basket of them,
and I cooked them for Celeste.
She smiled so sweetly as she ate
each spoonful and she told me
to make sure to come by to say
thank you, so here I am.

II: Run

Some days I am happy to be not me
                    — David St. John

Today I throw earth over the rough
cedar that holds the secret
of my laughter. He said he
loved the muscles in my thighs,
the way my shoulders took up
space; his hands would linger
on the top of my backside.
How we made love — talking
about it in code all day afterwards,
and how easy it was to feel
as if we had never stopped.
Once, he asked me to run —
me, a grown woman like me —
to run, not to catch a bus, not
from a storm, just to run
so he could see me run,
because he said he wanted
to see me run like I did
when I was a child, because
he'd missed that, and he wanted
to see it. So I ran, my breasts
bouncing, and we laughed
so hard, and he stood
open-armed so I could fill
him with my sweat and sweetness,
my laughter and my softening.
I gave him the small precious
fruit in me, and watched him eat
it slowly, his eyes on me steadily.

Today, Christ, I must cover him
with dirt; and sometimes I can't tell,
dear God, if it is you I am praying
to or him, and maybe this
is the idolatry of love that you
are saving me from, for what
I should feel is anger – after all,
he did leave my bed and bring home
a part of someone else that had
taken him and will take me, too.
And what has he left me with? Debts
to pay, a blank sky, a son full of questions,
and this thing in me. Yet, Lord,
I pray as if it is him listening.
Lord, forgive me for praying,
as I have, that he did not love
her enough to ask her to run
for him, giggling, falling, big-limbed
and heavy into his open arms.

III: *The Handmaiden*

> *You do what you do first then I do what I want to do*
> — William Carlos Williams

I am handmaiden to this flesh
that is wasting away quickly.
These days I have so little
time. I spend my days
counting these faded, sweat-soaked
gourdes smelling of people's meals, crotches,
held in my fists, let go reluctantly;
and cleaning what is left of him,
waiting for the smile he gives,
and then the tears – so much
crying. A part of me won't
stop to tell him that this
shadow of regret that haunts
him every time I wipe the shit
from his thighs is not his
lot, for something in me says
guilt is its own healing
and there is no time to stop
and promise him freedom.
I am the handmaiden of today;
tomorrow, you have said,
should take care of itself.
But, dear God, do this one thing
for me, handmaiden of the dying,
the marshal of the fading, the boatman
with a cooling rag and a soft song
for the crossing. Tomorrow may I
walk at dusk, my mouth moving,
under the yellow blossoms

of a ripe gingko tree, talking
to you? Lord, have mercy on our
poor unconscionable souls.

IV: Habitation

We will gather the remnants of this
habitation, then carry them where
the Spirit leads, this tent of the Lord,
somewhere where the stones did not
fall and the earth seems ready
for the planting of pegs and poles.
And in the cool blue light of sun
coming through the stretched
tarpaulin given to us by the Brazilian
men in blue helmets – they with
their big smiles, the offence of charm,
as if that alone can turn us into
stoic holy people – we are,
Lord, grateful and say, amen.

The congregation claps hands
as we stand on the dusty ground,
our skins clean with cupfuls
of rainwater, our clothes dusted
off, the white crushed marl
like dandruff where our arms
cannot reach; and we will sing,
for this is the habitation of the Lord.

The dead leave a space in us, and
this woman, this warrior on her knees,
armed with breastplate, shield, helmet
and sword, knows the purpose
of cataclysms. We are the remnant,
and we are here for no good reason
that comes from us, just the wisdom

of the Lord, just his providence,
his unknowable plan.

I could have been broken
by falling stones, but now I walk
in these streets, my mouth speaking
only that which is left to be spoken:
Prepare ye, the habitation of the Lord,
prepare ye the way for His coming.

V: Stone

Though she teaches me how to bear
the brute hurt we women carry,
though her garments are grace and forgiveness,
dear Lord, I know her nights are heavy
with regret. The thing she cannot
let go is the man who abandoned
her, took flight, made his money,
lived the American Dream, then returned
with one knapsack, a pocket full
of ash, and eyes so hollow, they
seemed as trusting as a child's.
She knew that the pall over his skin
was death, and though he did
not ask, she told him he would
have to die alone in the old stable
behind the maternity clinic.
She would not be there for him.
He died alone, and no
sadness overtook her, just this
stone she carries, a stone
she has always lied about.
Lord, I pray that even now,
that stone may turn to dust
to make a truth of her lie.

VI: Pastor

He towers over the congregation
as if their raised hands are lifting
him, this slight, tiny man
who will preach out a bleak
tale of retribution and fire,
the unwavering equation
of damnation. Once, I wondered
what hurt could make him throw
words at our bodies, the fear
rising from our crotches
and armpits, making us
stumble down the aisles,
to fall prostrate before the altar,
before this tiny man who stood
like a giant in the thick heat
of salvation. Who was this man,
with the tough ropy limbs
of a machete wielding farmer?
When they brought
him out to the dusty ante-
chamber of the church,
the air still electric with brimstone,
my heart sped, knowing
he would curse me for my blood,
for the sin that brought me here,
with a dying husband,
and the promise of death inside me –
because of our flesh, our
tyrannous flesh. But this small
man took my hands, looked
into my face, called my name,
and wept – his tears dropping

151

onto our fused hands, his voice
a deep groan of lament;
then he held me to him
as tongues soft as feathers
on my skin circled us;
this is the healing I longed for,
this is the grace I received.

VII: *Sisters in the Lord*

These skirt-wearing women, these
women of kerchiefs in bosoms,
these women of legs that have
walked mountains and valleys,
these women with arms strong
as branches, who have squeezed
soap and water from clothes,
wringing them clean, these women
who stand guard at dawn
on their knees, the prayers
returning to the holy place,
these women with wombs
that have carried flesh and stone,
these women of shared blood
tides, these women who come
into the steaming room with
the single naked light, and
the squeaky bed where bodies
have wrestled with desire
and death, these women
who stand around me, scented
with hair preparations, talcum
powder, these women
who draw near and let loose
the prophesy of hope,
it is they who put their hands
on me, call me chosen
and tell me they love me
despite the lesions on my skin.
Then waiting for my stomach
to hurl up the truth you
have seeded in me, these women

hear me cry, "I will not die,
I will not die, I will not die till my
work is done!"

VIII: *Absence*

We arrive a day later, our silent
prayers paving the way as we
pick our way through the great
lamentation – all around us the dumb
look of people unable to even ask
why, just wondering where next
after this – all our plans
turned to rubble. I try to remember
the scriptures of grace, but all
I hear is the promise of disasters,
the falling of stones from above,
the last things. We arrive to see
more sky than we ever saw.
Where shadows fell we see
only the stony glare of the sky.
A thick, still layer of dust
hangs above the mountain
of stone. Our crowd
has gathered, soft smiles at
the revenant of each other,
hearts caught in the threat
of absence. We whisper
names; some have answers,
most have no news. We have
rehearsed this wake for years,
rehearsed how to hold their
memory before us, but not like
this, not in such numbers,
not our two "ladies", the care-
takers of this building, the boys
who master make-up, the
Lazarus youth, the singing
dervishes, the flamboyant
beautiful long-limbed bodies.

X: Son

I know you are always preparing for it;
we have talked about sudden
death: a runaway truck, a motorcycle
taxi falling into a hole, cancer in
my breast, the floods of hurricanes,
and earthquakes; and we nod
as if agreeing that these things
could happen. But we know it's not
the same, it's not easy to forget
that you are my altar boy, a kind
of handmaiden waiting for the first
signs: a persistent cough, my
sluggish walk to the backyard
with a pan of water to wash.
How long will it take for me to do
the mathematics of white cells;
the number of days stretched
out waiting for the body to find
its way back? This is your legacy,
you, constant orphan, you
who walk through this world
with the abandonment of a lost
child. You listen to my plans
with indulgence and quiet
impatience, as if you know
something I do not.
Maybe you wonder why we
have given you this burden,
My son, I love you for being
such a willing orphan, carrying
my bags, holding my hand.
It is your lot; and these days,
all I can give in return
is this painful gratitude.

CINE

They make a cinema
in the hollow space of a hall
that survived it all.

We sit in the full, fleshy
dark and the world is so
far away. I am crying.

I am laughing. I am beautiful.
I forget tomorrow, yesterday.
Outside, the fallen stones wait.

THE CRACK

I: The Crack

I haven't measured the crack on
my wall, but I know it is the length
of my arm and just as skinny,
though for cracks in a wall
in an upper chamber above
abandoned ground floor rooms,
that is a fairly thick crack.

My wall is lime green – this is how
I found it when I moved here –
though at night, in the kerosene
light, it is a strange deep green
like the light one gets beneath
a mango tree at dawn. The crack
is already peeling at the edges,
and at dusk I can see the red
sun falling through the fissure.

At night I imagine it opening up,
letting the heavy ceiling
break apart, fall through,
crushing my lime green room.
I have tried sleeping in the tent
village in the centre of the city,
but my lungs get wet and thick,
and I cough painfully, knowing
how quickly I will die there.
There is all that sin around
so close I can smell it,
hear its sounds, feel its flesh

brushing me – so hard to be
holy in that place.

So I return to my room
and here I can die if He wants
me to, but then I am dying
anyway, a man walking around
with the crutch of grace – prophecies,
so many prophecies in my chest.

I have planted hibiscus flowers
and mint leaves inside my crack,
and I stuff it each day with the yellow
faded leaves of my old bible;
each rolled-up sheet of scriptures
placed in safekeeping
in my heart, a prayer for the living.

II: The Celibate

These days, the Celibate attracts
loose-limbed, dark-skinned women
of startling beauty, dressed in their

modest pastel-coloured dresses,
their powder-blue hats, their strong
leather shoes, dusty with walking

for miles through the city
with their gospel of peace, their
strong legs – such elegant calves –

gleaming with sweat and lotion
as they climb the side hills
of Port-au-Prince to the tiny

churches where congregations
of the hopeful praise Jesus.
These women are the acolytes

of the Celibate preacherman,
the itinerant prophet; they walk
by his side; they say very little;

they smile the smile of innocence;
they carry his sermons, some bottled
water, a peeled orange, a sandwich

for his lunch. It is they who
keep the money collected
in the offering plate. These days

his celibacy is a redundancy,
since everyone knows he is
one of those AIDS men – at least

this is what the people imagine
as they watch him walk with
these sisters of the Lord. But they

know him to be a man of such
fortitude that sometimes while
he waits on their porch to walk

them to the next service, they step
out and offer him a glass of water,
braless, with only a thin orange

slip separating him from their skin,
their heads covered with a bed-rag
to keep intact their perm. They

do this as if they have not considered
it, as if unaware of the immodesty
of it, the tease of it, as if they

are not testing the Celibate to see
if he will look beyond their faces.
And he has been constant, this

piece of wood, stern, all business –
though all women can tell when
a man's eyes are burning into their back,

when a man is looking at the sway
of their waist. This is how they know
him to be a man of such fortitude.

The women carry his secrets,
the things he has shared: the wife
he has hidden in the mountains,

the disease he has caught doing
the thing a celibate must not be seen
to have done. Now they imagine

him propped on his thin arms,
his lean back shiny with sweat,
moving, moving, his chiselled head

bobbing before the chaos of arrival,
just as it does when he preaches.
Jesus. This is the heaven of the Celibate,

the perk of the abstainer, the blessing
of this ailment, that he walks about
with women, beautiful tender women,

carrying in them the sweet secret
of their imaginings, for the sake
of the gospel, for the love of the Lord.

III: My Seed

Not one of my seed shall sit on the side-
walk and beg your bread, beg your coins,
beg your sip of water. Not one of my
seed shall stumble naked along these
roads of stone and dust searching
for the slippers of their mothers,
a piece of scarf, the hem of a dress,
or any clue that this is where
they last stopped – maybe to ask the time,
or to answer a phone call – there with a bag
of fish, eggplants, okras, tampons,
and a tiny bottle of wine in her hand
before the darkness fell. No, not one
of my seed shall sit on the corner
waiting to be jumped, knifed, robbed
of what little they have. Not one of my seed
shall hear the gospel of Christ
thickening the green morning and turn away,
only to walk to their untimely death
and face the judgment of the Lord.
Not one of my seed shall see this
country swallowed by catastrophe
and decay. No, not one of my seed
shall have to ask their mother why
she is a whore and a liar, why
she walks with eyes that do not see.
Not one of my seed shall sit
on the bed's edge and watch me,
their father, slowly waste away.
None of them will have to ask God
why he has left them bereft
of a father, with a broken home,

163

and then a squalid death to come.
Not one of my seed shall stand
in the dark and wait for the coming
of morning, not sure when or if
it will come. Not one of my seed
shall sin. Not one of my seed shall
curse me. Not one of my seed shall know
the curse of seedlessness. My seed shall stay
cocooned in my balls where they will
remain dry, blank and dumb.

MADAME

For Bebee

Still too pretty to fear her age,
the flesh on her is firm
in that settled way it grows
firm on women who have walked,
danced and rocked. She knows
her wounds have taught her
much: the man who could not
wait, pushing her into the shadows,
prying open her legs, slapping
away her hand with the condom,
his orgasm a fierce invective,
then quick withdrawal,
taking a fistful of sheet
to wipe himself before the tuck
away, the dig into his pocket,
and the showering of her body
with twenties – five hundred
dollars covering her as she bent
over to pull up her panties:
"Salot, goddamned whore!"
A week later she learns he is dead;
AIDS, they say. And then she
cries. This is the wisdom of
a street-walking woman – like when
to cross to the other side, when
to stay close enough to lights
that someone may hear the
voices and grunts in the shadows;
when to feign a fitful orgasm
so he will shudder in excitement
then grow flaccid and not petulant

with shame; when to laugh
and when not to laugh; when to
weep; when to quarrel and when
to lie still as a damp sheet
for the temper to pass.

At night she makes plans:
fifty gourdes from the teacher
at the school with beautiful
teeth and foul underarms; one-
fifty gourdes from the Argentine
water trader who will come cursing
sex in rapid Spanish; nothing
from the carpenter from Ganthier
who is old enough to become
a giver for the future – for him
she will profess love and offer him
bread and the last of the roasted
goat, a down-payment on better
days. Tomorrow's two meals
will be covered and her daughters
will have their porridge – sufficient
to the day. These days a saying
slips quietly off the tongues
of the living when the dead
return to their hearts like the dust
before rain: "I could have been
like you. God knows best" –
the fickle trick of this earth.
It is how she moves each day,
how she counts her coins,
how she pushes against the
thrusting man, how she closes
her eyes, how she sighs,

how she lets the nerves leap,
and then spread light over her
body, how she pants, how
she turns over to sleep
another day, a song dancing
in her head, spilling from her
mouth, before the nonsense
worlds of dreams cover her.

SAVA?

We no longer ask, *Sava?*
We are carrying too many gloomy answers
on our backs these days, and no matter

how much we try to unburden ourselves,
they cling to us. So we mumble, *Bon jour* —
like a soft prayer, really — then we hurry on.

SHELTERED

It's here also that all the dust coming from the houses
says good-morning to the dead
as if nothing happened.
 — George Castera

The shelter of mango trees,
the familiar haze of corn fields,
the scent of wood-fire,
the amplified voice of the *predicateur*
carrying over the trees:
the language dances to me,
then slips away. I hear its soul
in the tune, the flattened
vowels, the sharp, alert consonants,
and the laughter. Here is
the comfort of tombstones, the dead
sealed in near the house, as if
another bivouac has been built here,
as if the million displaced bodies
have joined another million
displaced souls searching
for a place to lay their heads,
as if the living know to make room
for the souls of the wandering dead.
A raffia chair is set on the soft
cement dust at the foot
of the pink and powder-blue
mausoleum, a favourite chair
she will come back to in the cool
of the evening, just to be among
them. In the morning,
before the first sip of fresh coffee,

the dark sweetness is poured
generously into the earth
of their graves to cut the early chill.
If the Lord says you must continue
along this path, that you must
take up your metal folding
chair and walk through the bushes
to the main road where believers
are clapping hands and beating
tambourines, then you know
that is what you must do –
these deals you have made with love,
with God's purposes – and you pray
for the gift you know is needed
by those who walked out of the dust,
bodies intact, minds crushed, hearts quivering.
It must keep you walking, your body
upright, the planting of your legs
that have carried what all Haitian
women have carried – the buckets
of water, the black pots, the bundles
of wood, the limp bodies of sleeping
babies, picking your way over the stones,
moving towards the shelter
where the congregation raises
holy hands and waits for first light.

BEBE'S WISH

When you leave here, head down
Canape Vert to your cool hotel room,
to the breadfruit casserole and barbecue
chicken, to the closed-in peace of your
life, say my name to Bon Dieu, say
the name Bebe – he is going to look
for me somewhere in Petion Ville
in the courtyard of L'ecole de la Republica
de Guatemala, behind the low white
wall, in a crowd of blue tarpaulin
huts, he will find me laughing, singing
something by Beyonce or maybe
an old hymn while pouring water
over my head in the piss-smelling
concrete alcove where we get clean.
He will see me earning my keep;
from above, what he'll see
is the clumsy back of a man
hurrying to pour his waiting into
me, then the casual slip off,
the counting of gourdes, the talk
of family, the football score –
not tomorrow, maybe Thursday,
will you be free at three?...
And Bon Dieu will hear me say something
tender, my voice trying to leave him
with just enough to look back
and see me as a girl, all new,
so he will come back, so he will
see me as lovely, even
when he is confessing to the priest.
Bon Dieu will find me greasing

my hair, and he will know it is me,
Bebe, by my spirit, because it is all
I have now. Tell me, before you go,
what do you think I am worth, eh?
Tell me how much you would
pay for me, for just a piece of me
to take back with you, not
so much that your bags will be
too heavy on the flight, just enough
to slip in your pocket,
so that wherever you are,
you can take me out and sniff
me, remembering me. How much
for that part of me that must stay
lovely, sweet, the part that sees
in men's hands the promise of more?
How much would you pay? Today,
I charged fifty gourdes for him
take me from behind, quick, short,
over in minutes, then he jumped
on the bike he was so worried about
he parked it inside my tent.
Fifty gourdes. He was a taxi man
with exact change, who said my name –
Bebe, Bebe!, like you cheer a good
football team. Was that enough?
Tonight, if I get a hundred
for a transaction in the alley
with the high hedge at the Digicel Building,
I will kiss him on the lips, give
him twenty gourdes back in change,
telling him to come back.
Is that enough? What will God
tell you to give me? Remember me,

Bebe, with the full mouth of Africa,
the shape of an almond; Bebe,
whose eyes know how to laugh
with sadness; Bebe, whose titties
still stand tall, Bebe; queen of the
sugar walk; Bebe waving you goodbye.
Maybe next time you come
I will tell you that he did come by,
Bon Dieu, to see me, to tell me
how much I should ask for,
how much you will pay for this,
for all of this right here.

GANTHIER

I thought, he said of the wife,
who stayed six months until
the news of this treachery of the
blood, before he lay on his back,
the bottles of toxic drugs and poison
for rats lined up on his sill,
before the equation of fatigue
with this world, a body falling to ruin,
a heart shattered by a woman's laughter,
I thought before she left, the woman
of beauty who knew her beauty,
I thought, he said, she was an angel,
but she wasn't – as sometimes
happens. But now – he smiled
that lazy trickster grin, his
amber eyes sparkling – he's found
his archangel; and this is how
a cliché for a pop song
becomes a hymn for saints.
She came and saved him,
the way archangels come into
a room – not asking permission,
walking in wingless as if they have
an army of angels at their command –
like the scent of incense filling
your breath and anointing you.
And you fall in line. This is
bigger than love. A book,
an apocryphal book with chapter
and verse, could be written
about this thing – the voice
of God commanding

the mystery of celestial beings
sacrificed as the mates
of flesh-weak humans – she
is this archangel with a wound
in her body – as if the whole
thing was planned: *I will
place a curse on you, something
haunting, something reserved
for the damned, the thin bodies
sprawled out in the shadows
whispering, straining for air.
I will let her carry this disease,
and then I will command you
to marry her, take her as your wife,
and you will learn how much bigger
than desire love is, how much
wider than hunger.*
                              He looked
at her, lying there on her stomach
on the mattress covered in a white
sheet, out there on the porch
where the air is cooler,
dressed in her pink church
skirt suit, looking at him, having
fed him, given him water to drink,
poured water for his hands,
and he said, "I do not deserve
her, her name should be grace;
I do not deserve this shelter,
and I ask her all the time,
'Why do you love me?' And she
says, 'It is bigger than me and you,'
and that is all she says. Maybe
a man must always wait to touch

the flesh of an archangel,
and come to it as to an altar.
A man must not let the light
in her eyes fool him into thinking
this is ordinary flesh. A man must wait
to marry her properly, give her
a ring, give her the laughter
of a family gathered. A man must
do all these things before he falls
prostrate before the body of
of an archangel who does not
even know she is divine,
except in the way a vessel
knows it is set aside for pure
water. This is how love is for those
cursed with the love of archangels.

GUINEP

At the end of the guinep
is the white seed,
brittle as an egg.

She sucks fiercely,
her teeth dragging
off the orange flesh.

The stain and sweet
is the only sure way
to settle her nausea.

She has waited long
for the season
to come with the rains.

At the end of a body
is the bald seed,
the bone, white as egg.

FLAKES

Our dawns drown in ashes
— Michel-Ange Hyppolite

The first flakes dance
in the wind, then when
the air grows still
they fall lightly,
covering our skins.

At first it is hard
to see the grey on the ground,
though above us
the crowd of darkness hangs.

At dusk, raise your nose,
you will pick out
the scent of hardwood,
stewed chicken and onions.

At dusk raise your nose,
you will smell soap and talc,
you will smell the piss on the wall,
the waste of suffering.

The sirens make a half-
hearted wail, and then stop;
the smoke keeps pouring
out of the ruined house.

Someone is walking home
to a crowd, to a dry carcass
of a house, to flakes falling
softly on her face.

She read a poem once about
snow on grass, how it gathers
and turns everything white.
Tomorrow she will

find shelter under a blue
tarpaulin, and everything
around her will be blue
as the undersea.

PARAKEET

Against a wall at Champ de Mars
you buy a caged parakeet;
Hispaniola, the book says,
green and gregarious.
It will talk to you, they promise.
You ask how long
it will last. Forever,
the hustler says; just
feed it corn and birdseed,
or drop a mango
and some dead flies
in the cage and it will
live for longer
than you can love it.

You take the bird home,
hang the cage
from the mango tree
in the courtyard,
and it shits green and grey
on the white rubble
of your neighbours' home,
and sings all day,
so that the street
sounds like a forest.
You tell Celeste
that when the bird dies,
you will not be far
behind.

The air in the office
is too cold these days,
and you run to the toilet
to cough so hard your body
aches with the effort,
and you wonder
what a cage will do
to a parakeet,
or what the rain
gathering over the hills
will do to the bird.
You think that sometimes
your body has grown
so light it could lift
and fly.

Celeste says, don't grow
attached. She says she read
that parakeets will die
in a year, no more.
And you smile and say
that is what you thought,
and throw a rotting
mango in the cage
just to watch the green
parakeet tug brown
and orange meat
into its beak.
Mesmerized by her,
you wonder how old
she was when you
bought her.

THE FAST

Today, he says, miracles will bloom:
four days of water and air, and now,
dizzy with visions, he says, today, today.

The *predicateur* prays for a plate of beans
and steamed rice for the woman curled
in the shadows, breathing painfully.

Today, he says, miracles will bloom:
this one cometh only by prayer and fasting.
My life, he smiles, should be a mansion of miracles.

WOMB

My womb is a graveyard. I have cursed it.
My sons, do not look at my womb;
it will make you blind.

The dark shadow of your beginning
is the face of death. My womb
is a graveyard, so many dead.

My beautiful sons, I wish I could
return you to the shelter of my womb,
hold you in my eggs forever.

My soft-eyed sons, will you forgive me
for what I have done? Promise me
you will bury me.

Promise me I will not bury you,
promise me you will forgive
my treacherous womb.

MOTHER OF MOTHERS

When a brave woman's out walking
she's Mistress Life's spitting image
                    — Michel-Ange Hyppolite

The mothers of mothers
march through the congregation
while the children of men
clap their hands, beat
tambourines, scratch the grater
and sing the flat harmony
that shivers the air.

Beneath a cascade of flame-yellow
and red flamboyants,
they stalk the outskirts of the
feet-worn worship ground,
where the weeds and stones
have accumulated, where
the excavation of rubble takes
us as far as weary arms
and the creaky wheelbarrow
can go.

They draw a pattern
of circles with their heavy planted
feet, their arms raised high, their
voices continuing with greater
ceremony and occasion
the conversation that began
with Jesus at four in the morning.

Oh, the mothers of mothers,
who know too well the hottest
sorrow: how much a casket weighs,
how it feels on the open palm,
the broken bodies
of children – the boy who covers
a jaw full of maggots, and the
lanky son, whose spine
gave under the weight of concrete
before he was pulled out,
laid under the soft blue light
of a wayside clinic, waiting
to go, and quietly, with the flies
returning to his skin,
still, though he must wait
there until dusk, before they
notice, before a procession
of mothers leads the body out
into the night and, mother of
a son, she hears her child
wake, look around, and say:
"How nice the air is out here,"
before he dies, this time for good.

Mothers of mothers,
in your bandanas and with your
holy testaments, cheek bones
gleaming against taut skins,
eyes glazed, you must
draw the line of defence
around beleaguered souls,
and speak a torrent of curses
on the beast lurking in the shadows.

4

HOME, AGAIN

AT THE ALLEY'S ENTRANCE

Before I take you down this gloomy alley
whose mouth is rotted and seeping with green
slime from an open sewer, I want you
to look around you. You will see that at your
back is a sky so blue it makes you dumb
to talk of storm. Stretched below it
is the undulating mint and *callaloo* green
of canefields folding to the wind.
If you breathe deeply, you will smell
mud, the sharp astringence of the ocean,
and the sweet scent of a broken leaf.
I want you to remember all of this,
to remember the paved road we took
to get here, the old church-lady in her fruit-
filled hat and pale tan stockings, who
waved as we passed. Remember how
at first you were afraid before you
saw the way the sun cleared up
the dark shadows of the pre-dawn.
Remember all this, for down this alley
we will meet the symbol of all fear
and the sweet simplicity of desire.
You will know her name and forget
yours, and the shadow of your hunger
will consume you. Now let's go – she
is singing to us. Look askance. Trod sof'.

PORTENT

For Helen Vendler

This coming together of blanched bones
is verb, pure verb, like that guiltless
frolic of childhood – the way we recount
the things we used to do: eat leaves,
scoop tadpoles from stagnant ponds, swing
bats, fling stones into the thud-belly
of yelping dogs, peek through the slats
of louvres into the dusky room where
Merle's white bra glowed like a gash
of light on a bare mountain's face.
Sometimes the visions young men have
are stony portents of a frail future;
they stand like facades against the blue
day, granite-heavy, unmoving things.
And the air is stiff around them.
These days gerunds and past participles,
the grammar of pluperfects,
and the grammar of missed chances
condemn us – as if judgment has come.
But old men dream dreams, lie still
as planks on the cold ground,
hear the rattle of bones moving,
see them gathering, circling, finding
each other, making something new
in the graveyard of memory.
At forty-four, I long for dreams
that move, that pluck verbs
from the air and build battalions
of skeletons fit to dig digits into
the soil, bring up mud to plaster
over the frame, until the clay
hardens into something gleaming.

ONCE

...I should be glad of another death...
T.S. Eliot

It is better to be the messenger of wrath,
the one chosen to announce the fury
of the avenger, than to admit to a hunger
for vengeance. Better, and so much easier
on memory. Think of old Mother Miller
who will sit, ankles crossed like a good
trained teacher should, for hours staring
at nothing, her mind recording nothing,
before she, with limbs cracked like sun-dried
ashy sticks scattered in the salty air of
Clarendon's dry flatlands, suddenly says,
for the fifth time in an hour: *We pass*
this way but once... You know that memory
gem? You know that memory gem?
We pass this way but once. Then she stops.
To remember one's enemies
is to carry the canker of pain in the skin;
soon the brain will not contain the hurt,
and a blackness arrives softly. Better
to be told that a curse is upon so and so,
that such and such mountain shall fall,
that this or that nation shall crumble,
shall eat itself, vomit and swallow,
than to speak as if these things were
harvested in your heart. At dusk, she walks
past me, she has forgotten my face.
I might be the enemy or the ally –
it does not matter – we pass this way
but once and beyond is that quiet

191

place of rest. *To go forward*, she tells me,
is to die. Better to wait now, useless,
a soft silence upon you, waiting to simply
slip away, where the enemies are not.

A COMPLEX AGELESS LONGING

For Neville Dawes

The cassia flowers bloom a startling yellow
in the branches' shelter; every blue light
turns a mellow breath and brown ska thumps
where Kingston is cooler, deep in the shade.
Imagine a prophet stepping out of tendril
roots and dangling flowers like fruit;
imagine her expanding her arms
and speaking through lips lined white
with fasting, imagine this as a way
to understand the hills, the way they purple,
then blue to something charcoal and old
when the mist falls on them: then
you will have understood the calculation
of faith, not doctrine. Under the soft
topography of fluid light, a white-
dressed prophet, her body dark
and knotted, her breasts like stones
against the stiff fabric of her garment,
is the icon of an island. The tabernacle
warns us to listen and do, tells us
that all seed planted and watered,
though fresh, will die in this barren ground
where stones multiply and shards
of smashed bottles glint in the bare
light. Prodigy saints – that coterie
of precocious, tongue-speaking infants –
step out of the shelter of the cassia
full-grown, their eyes hungry
for the light on the hills.
Despite this we find poems
written by an apostate father full

of gospel and faith. Now his death
is a mystery. Perhaps the half
has not yet been told. Perhaps we may
speak on the other side, the things
of soft soil, quiet hills and the loam
of old villagers, that churchgoing
tribe of black folks who move at dawn
like gashes of white against the gloom.

UPON OUR 14TH ANNIVERSARY
for Lorna

We drive through the irregular curves and dips
of Kingston's suburbs, deep craters, cluttered gullies
cutting through roads. Adjoa's tiny car is a shelter
of laughter and the making of nostalgia. We know
people die on these streets all the time – but tonight
we are able to forget. We spend thirty minutes
making nonsense of the rituals of violence,
and for a day we recall the paths of our love,
the brick porch where I sang songs into the night,
the hall's spine I walked up to see you in the powder-
blue frock, your smile – the first hit of a chronic
addiction I still tremble for all these years later.
Sometimes home is a poem of lament, but tonight
we see Kingston as a freshly painted world of chaos,
a kind of giddy playground. So that after the steamed
snapper and gummy bammy, the coconut water
and guava-pineapple juice at the Fish Place
on the decent end of Constant Spring Road,
Adjoa's car is filled with our children so loud
with playground laughter and the sweetness
of children teetering on the edge of rudeness,
singing Julio Iglesias and Simon and Garfunkel.
We marvel at Kekeli's deep baritone –
him just barely eleven – holding on to each
note's curve as he anchors Paul Simon's thin voice
until we arrive safely, feeling groovy, at West Road.
We sit in the dark until the last guitar strum
and our voices have settled into the hum of joy:
and I understand, again, why I love you, I love us.

THE WAY OF LOVE

In the pride of your heart you say,
"I am a god; I sit in the throne of a god in the heart of the seas."
                                                        (Ezekiel 28:2)

Glance at the brown shadow of a man,
the protrusion of his belly, the firm
slope of his groin, before the dense
shrubbery, like the entanglement of leaves
before the branches. See this and imagine
that a man with hands large as love
could grow bloated in his glory,
so much that he falls easily
to the rigid tyranny of desire.
I love a brother like I do the grotesque
lump of my ankle, the one crushed
by a hit-and-run car, the one that smarts
with its own indulgence late at night.
It is mine despite its constant betrayals,
and I have come to know the awkward
beauty in its warped shape.
A brother-friend will not confess his fall,
the simple truth that with his open
palm he has beaten his woman,
the one he loves, beaten her so that
the night after the terror, the lie
was a nervous stone in the room,
as if confession would have been
the beginning of all dissolutions.
This is the way men grow false —
the silent conspiracy of our
boyhood agreements: the code of avoidance,
the cool of tolerance, while a rot sets in.

HOME, AGAIN

The island is nervous, a twitchy rhythm
shaking the flamboyant; the city
is brighter here, neurotic as the army
of crack beggars – used to be that mad men
understood the nuance of rejection.
The crackhead on Dunrobin Avenue
looks like an old school friend.
He stands staring, hands out pleading.
You can smell the stink on him,
like rotten fruits and a chafed crotch.
He rejects the stray mongrel's
instinct for personal space.
Ah, my rebel city! The cars
lean into turns, find the rhythm
of advantage, a blaring horn, a rush
of wheels, the alarm of brake-lights.
We obey the rules now, not for fear
of retribution by the law, but like trained
animals, skittish and wary of the broken
red light. Chris complains of the *chi-chi*
men invading Emancipation Park,
speaks of summary execution
of *chi-chi* men as the dying spasm of a nation
succumbing to the lax laws of Mammon
and Uncle Sam. At the Courtleigh
Manor Hotel, a wizened murderer
tells his saga late into the night:
the man he stabbed, the years in GP,
the buggery like eating, the terror,
the dumb bewilderment of his release,
entering the schizophrenic city,
wanting to crawl back into the jail

to die there. He talks as if shed blood
is nothing between friends. We laugh
easily and women smile, their musky scent
thickening the night with the ferment
of their heat. My brothers flank me.
We are middle-aged now and talk
of weight, exercise, bum knees,
of betraying blood and vanishing hair.
We warm to each other. All those years.
Then sleep comes in this Kingston
like poems will on a humid night,
to the relay of dogs and the deejay
riding roughshod over the bass-line:
everything barely held together.

HEART

I am growing a new heart: flesh
and that fragile basket of veins, twisting
a wise galaxy of lines all over
the old fat gulping thing. These days
the calcification of dogma, the old
cement of ideology has crumbled.
Blame the tramping of news stories,
the blood on glossy screens, the wail
of friends bedlamized by the blast
of indiscriminate viciousness – and soldiers
returning inert. I know that blood
and its shedding are the discourse
of nations, and I have grown
a heart that can feel the wearying
gloom of hopelessness. People die.
Smooth-faced Kyle killed himself
on Thanksgiving eve at the news
that we knew he stole words
from a stranger, and his father,
with a fat gold ring in his left ear,
wanders the campus hoping to catch
a whisper of him in the Autumn air.
A man who slaughtered hundreds
has ripped out his heart,
stared at its pulsing glow
and then smashed it into the ground.
The question returns: *Why?*
Now my tendril heart no longer
calls it ordinary madness, instead,
it pumps, stays meaty, fresh,
pliant, vulnerable to all sadnesses.

CITY

for Kingston

It is different when you know
the give of summer-hot asphalt
eating away the thin barrier
between your soles and perdition.
It is different when in the still air
the smell of rotting meat cooking
to a ripeness suffocates you.
It is different when you can't tell
the decay of things around you
from your own stench; the way
fresh sweat loosens old indiscretions,
your fingernails turning black
with wet mud and dead skin
when you scratch your crotch.
It is different when you have lost
count of the dead by gunshot
or some idiotic medieval stab wound
or a body crushed by a truck –
so painless the departure of souls.
It is different when you know,
as the prophet did, that the city
is a cooking pot and we its exiles
are the stewing meat, for you know,
like breathing, that the end is nearer.
Which is not much different, really;
but it is something, anyway.

CLARA

Clara walks along West Liberty,
past Swan Lake and its rituals
of middle-class splendour, turning
the corner into the treeless glare
of that broken graveyard where the slain
negroes have lain for centuries.
Someone has told her to talk to the dead.
Beneath a blasted, live oak tree,
Clara starts to talk in a whisper that is picked
up by a simple wind, taken up high
with the dried leaves, until she can shout
to fight it all, and the bones turn in the dirt.
Clara shouts from her belly till her chest
strains with air and her throat grows gravelly.
A storm rises in the East, a big bluster
of sound like the blast of demolition or the storm
of bombs at dusk. Clara trembles
in the slash of rain and light, watching
grey bones turn white and luminescent
in the gloom. The storm clatters away
leaving the earth wet, and the voice says:
Call to breath, let breath come. It comes
like a silk cloth over skin. She hears the grass
growing softly from the soil, stretching
gently. She hears the ants busying themselves
along their old paths to the rot of flesh,
all of them waiting to be consumed by light,
the light of bones, a flaming, the grace
of new dawns at the breaking of old graves.

Swan Lake, Sumter, SC

SKETCH

With graphite I soften your bones,
make exotic the absence of your lash.
Your fingers – neat, elegant –
cradle a plum, the light of its juice
flaming vermillion through the taut skin.

I etch out your gaze, tender, tender
about your forehead, where the howl
of darting pain creases all. Softly,
as if with the soft lead, I can calm
it all, make it go away. You are going.

With the press of my palm's heel
I caress the bald glow of your head,
then clean a grey line where your brows
were – now there is nothing –
these markings of what you have suffered.

These days, bodies crumble
about me; the dead, desperate for healing,
grow weary, stoic, then quietly go.

My blackened fingers make things round –
you plump as a fruit just plucked.
Tomorrow I lift you, bird of bones,
your limbs collapsed.

There is sunlight crawling across the lawn.
Despite the drought, it's resiliently green,
except the narrow path of old sod we laid,
traumatized by neglect into a crude buzz-cut;
and this too is a symbol of our loss.

It is August in Columbia. Nothing can fight in this heat. Just stay still; maybe a small wind will blow, maybe a small wind.

SOME RANDOM NOTES

The poems in "Wheels" are meditations on the *Book of Ezekiel* and Gabriel Garcia Marquez's *Living to Tell the Tale*.
"Eat" from *Ezekiel 3*
"Rituals Before the Poem" from *Ezekiel 4*
"Baldness" from *Ezekiel 5*
"Genocide, Again" from *Ezekiel 6*
"Wise man" from *Ezekiel 13*
"The End has Come" from *Ezekiel 7*
"Dry Bones" from *Ezekiel 38*

"Last Days" – epigraph from Alan Ginsberg's "Angelic Black Holes".

The poems in "The Measure" were commissioned by the BBC for the programme, "Lion of Judah, Gentleman of Bath" (producer, Julian May), which aired in October 2005.

The poems in "Brimming" are a dialogue with the art of Brian Rutenberg – NY-based South Carolina artist. These poems, commissioned by the USC Atelier Program and the South Carolina State Museum, were published in the chapbook, *Brimming*, (Stepping Stone Press, 2006) "Brimming" was performed at the South Carolina state Museum in August 2006.:

"Dreaming of St. Augustine" – after "Spanish Moss" – thanks also to Kevin Smith for his history of the Stono Rebellion of 1738.
"How to Pick a Hanging Tree" – after "Shade"
"Lost in Enoree County" – after "After Rain"
"Brimming"– after "Waccamaw #28
"Gone Fishing" – after "Enoree # 11"
"River Love" – after "Santee # 41"
"Graves" – after "Irish Painting #15"
"Peach Wine and Political Poetry" – after "Oceanides #8
"Shelter" – after "Sanctuary #2"
"On Landscape Painting and Pioneers" – after "Algonquin"

"Carolina Gold" – after "Carolina Gold"

Poems in "Thunder in the Egg" emerged from a period of over a year while I was a correspondent for the Pulitzer Center on Crisis Reporting, reporting on HIV AIDS in Haiti after the tragic earthquake of January 2010. These poems are a homage to the people I met on my many trips to Port au Prince in 2010, and owe much of their energy to the amazing photography of Andre Lamberston.

Poems collected in this book have first appeared in some form in various publications including:

The Southern Poetry Anthology
NW15: The Anthology of New Writing, Volume 15
Moving Worlds
Caribbean Review of Books
Home Is Where
MaComere
PBS News Hour

ABOUT THE AUTHOR

Born in Ghana in 1962, Kwame Dawes spent most of his childhood and early adult life in Jamaica. As a poet, he is profoundly influenced by its rhythms and textures, citing in a recent interview his "spiritual, intellectual, and emotional engagement with reggae music." His book, *Natural Mysticism*, explores that engagement.

He has published seventeen collections of poetry, two poetry anthologies, three works of fiction, four works of non-fiction and a play. His essays have appeared in numerous journals including *Bomb Magazine*, *The London Review of Books*, *Granta*, *Essence*, *World Literature Today* and *Double Take Magazine*.

A collection of his plays will come out in 2012.

Until July 2011, Dawes was Distinguished Poet in Residence, Louis Frye Scudder Professor of Liberal Arts and founder, and executive director of the South Carolina Poetry Initiative. He was the director of the University of South Carolina Arts Institute and is the programming director of the Calabash International Literary Festival, which takes place in Jamaica in May of each year. Dawes is currently the Glenna Luschei Editor of *Prairie Schooner* at the University of Nebraska, where he is a Chancellor's Professor of English, a faculty member of Cave Canem, and a teacher in the Pacific MFA Program in Oregon.

In 2009 he won an Emmy Award in the category New Approaches to News and Documentary Programming: Arts, Lifestyle and Culture for his work on www.LiveHopeLove.com, a multimedia website on the human face of HIV/AIDS in Jamaica. It was this project that inspired the collection *Hope's Hospice*, 2009.

RECENT TITLES BY KWAME DAWES

Hope's Hospice
ISBN: 9781845230784, pp. 64; pub. 2009; £7.99

While on assignment for the *Virginia Quarterly Review* to report on the impact of HIV/AIDS on Jamaica, Kwame Dawes could not prevent himself from writing poems in response to the stories he heard. In a way journalism is not designed to do, these poems pare away detail to reveal the truths of character and situation, and find forms which both give expression to and find a kind of perfection for fleeting, difficult lives. These poems became, in time, this, his fourteenth collection of verse.

Powerfully illustrated by Joshua Cogan's photographs, the art of Dawes's poems makes it impossible to see HIV/AIDS as something that only happens to other people, and to marginalise their lives. Here, the experience of the disease becomes the channel for dramas that are both universal and unique, voices that are archetypal and highly individual – stories of despair and stoicism, deception and self-honesty, misery and joy in life.

Back of Mount Peace
ISBN: 9781845231248, pp. 91; pub. 2010, £8.99

A retired fisherman, Monty Cupidon, encounters a naked, bloodied and traumatised woman standing at the cross-roads. He offers comfort and takes her in. Suffering from amnesia, she cannot tell him anything about herself. The only clues are the signs that she has once worn a wedding ring, has a butterfly tattoo and red nail polish on her toes. In the absence of memory, he names her Esther. So begins a remarkable sequence of poems that explores many dimensions of liminality. *Back of Mount Peace* occupies a space between lyric and narrative, between reflection and story. It explores the space between body and mind, making Esther's halting discovery of her self through her body, which like a tree bears its indelible history and, unlike the mind, 'doesn't forget its grievances', work both as a moving narrative device and a deeply sensed and sensual reminder of the physicality of existence. Above all, this is a sequence that explores a relationship which begins in a primal Edenic space of innocent discovery in which, as Monty hopes, 'the hallelujah's of new love will begin', but which, like all relationships must enter history, the decay of time and the corruptions of knowledge.

Bivouac
ISBN: 9781845231057; pp. 196; pub. 2010; £9.99

When his father dies in suspicious circumstances, Ferron Morgan's trauma is increased by the conflict within his family and his father's friends over whether the death is the result of medical negligence or a political assassination. Ferron has lived in awe of his father's radical commitments but is forced to admit that, with the 1980s' resurgence of the political Right in the Caribbean, his father had lost faith, and was 'already dead to everything that had meaning for him'.

Ferron's response to the death is further complicated by guilt, particularly over his recent failure to protect his fiancée, Dolores, from a brutal rape. He begins, though, to investigate the direction of his life with great intensity, in particular to confront his instinct to keep running from trouble.

This is a sharply focused portrayal of Jamaica at a tipping point in its recent past, in which the private grief and trauma condenses a whole society's scarcely understood sense of temporariness and dislocation. For both Ferron and the society there has been the loss of 'the corpse of one's origins' and the novel points to the need to find a way back before there can be a movement forward.